The Lean, Brown Men

Main column advance.

Kwa-Direnna Position.

LUKIGURA RIVER.

The Lean, Brown Men

Experiences in East Africa During the
Great War with the 25th Royal Fusiliers
—the Legion of Frontiersmen

Angus Buchanan

LEONAUR

The Lean, Brown Men: Experiences in East Africa During the Great War
with the 25th Royal Fusiliers—the Legion of Frontiersmen
by Angus Buchanan

First published under the title
Three Years of War in East Africa

Published by Leonaur Ltd

Text in this form and material original to this edition
copyright © 2008 Leonaur Ltd

ISBN: 978-1-84677-482-9 (hardcover)
ISBN: 978-1-84677-481-2 (softcover)

http://www.leonaur.com

Contents

Foreword   7

Preface   15

Outward Bound   17

Frontier Life   28

Cattle Raiders   48

The First Advance   63

The Second Trek   79

The Third Stage   111

The End of the Campaign on German Soil   147

Nature Notes   168

Here and Hereafter   190

Foreword

Captain Buchanan has done me the honour of asking me to write a short preface to a work which seems to me at all events of peculiar interest. To write a preface is a difficult task, unless one has some real *raison d'être* for the task; yet I find it difficult to refuse, if only for my intense admiration for the part played by the battalion with which the author was so long and honourably associated—the 25th Royal Fusiliers.

The author's qualifications to write this work are undoubted, not only from his stout record as a soldier, but also through his previous experience as a traveller, explorer, and student of Natural History. When war broke out Captain Buchanan was engaged on behalf of the Provincial Government of Saskatchewan, Canada, in investigating the country in the far north, west of Hudson Bay, and studying and collecting the rarer flora and fauna. He had been for nearly a year many hundreds of miles out of touch with any other white man. The first rumour of war did not reach him until the end of October, when he at once struck south to a Hudson Bay Fort, which he reached at Christmas. Without delay he left to join up, and in but a month or two had changed his habitat from almost the Arctic Circle to the Equator.

Readers will be able to follow the fortunes of that wonderful unit, the 25th Royal Fusiliers, through the campaign, and will perhaps gain thereby an insight into this strangest of all side-shows more true and illuminating than a more comprehensive work. There was little that this old Legion of Frontiersmen missed. Comparisons are odious; yet I think it may safely be said that no other white unit took so full a part in the diverse stages of the campaign. They bore the long and arduous months of frontier and railway guarding in 1915. They took no mean share in the spectacular capture of Bukoba. Their mounted infantry as well as ordinary rank and file, took part in many of the small but intensely trying patrols through the thorny scrub along the Serengeti plains. General Smuts's operations around Kilimanjaro saw them. Right to the fore were they in the long and tiring treks, varied by frequent and fierce rear-guard actions, which took place down the Pangani and southward through the bush and forests to the capture of Morogoro; and onwards again right down to the Rufiji. They bore that cruelly hard period through the rains of 1916, when they held the Mgeta line against a numerically superior foe, living literally in a swamp for months, riddled through and through with fever. In January, 1917, when General Smuts made his final effort to crush the opposition, Colonel Driscoll and his men were right in the van, and here among others they lost Captain Selous, that great hunter and greater English gentleman. After a brief period in the south we find them back in time for the final stages of the campaign. Here they went in from Lindi to take part in the fighting of 1917, fighting so bitter that all the previous work was but as child's play in comparison. Lest it seem that I exaggerate, let me say that, with a force of about half the size, the casualties during these last four months were three times as great as those throughout the whole previous two years. There was indeed hardly an action in which the battalion did not take part, until that day on the 18th of October, 1917, when, while covering a temporary retirement, they were overwhelmed by immensely superior numbers and cut to pieces.

The author does not harp over-much on the sickness and

privations of his comrades—he has been through too many of them to do so; but I am reminded of the remark of one of them during the not infrequent periods of grousing which every respectable British soldier must have. "Ah, I wish to h—l I was in France! There one lives like a gentleman and dies like a man, here one lives like a pig and dies like a dog." There may have been something in this remark, yet I have thought as I saw the 25th staggering on, absolutely in rags, many with fever actually on them, nearly all emaciated and staring-eyed, that they were living, if not like gentlemen, at all events like *men*.

There is one point of view that I would like to put before readers in estimating the debt that those of us *who live in Africa* owe to these men—and that is this: when once the coastal belt was reached, and after the departure of General Smuts and practically all his South African fighting troops, it became apparent that European infantry, generally speaking, could no longer compete on even terms with the native soldier. The handicap of climate became too great. The European could no longer stand marching under a load, and more than that, the continual fever and sun sapped the *essential guts*, so that it became *almost* impossible for white troops to meet the German-African troops—led, of course, by trained and well-fed German officers and N.C.O.s—with any fair prospect of success. Such a fact boded ill for the future prestige of the white race. Yet it may be said that the Fusiliers soared triumphant even over this handicap; and they can boast, without fear of contradiction, that up to the very end no German field company would look with other than apprehension to meeting the 25th on even terms. I have always felt that the prowess and endurance of these fine men during these last months have done more to uphold our prestige and ensure the firm future of our rule than is likely to be adequately realised.

An estimate of the campaign as a whole is scarcely yet possible. It will probably be years before a just view can be taken of a side-show that is believed to have cost more money and many more lives than the whole of the South African Campaign. Many mistakes were made, and it is more than possible that the lion's share of what credit posterity may have to bestow will fall on Von Lettow and his comrades. Yet there were many factors which caused the task which Generals Tighe, Smuts, Hoskins, and Van Deventer did eventually accomplish, to be of almost unparalleled difficulty.

The question asked very often, and one which is likely to be of interest to posterity, is: How were the Germans able to prolong their resistance and, in fine, to make such a determined struggle against our very superior forces? In answer the following points seem to merit consideration.

In the first place the enemy had in the person of Colonel Von Lettow an outstanding personality, and a soldier whose merit it is hard to over-estimate. It will, moreover, always form one bright spot on the blackened German escutcheon that in his operations during the campaign, personally speaking, his conduct was as clean as it was efficient.

When war broke out the local military position was overwhelmingly in favour of the Germans. They had ready, at a conservative estimate, 2,000 to 3,000 trained whites and 8,000 native troops, with some 70 machine-guns and 40 guns. Against this we, on our side, had in British East Africa about 700 native soldiers and 2 machine-guns, one of which was out of action, and not more than 100 whites with any military experience at all. This force might possibly have been duplicated in Nyasaland. With this early crushing superiority it is obvious that expansion on the one side was easy—on the other a matter of extraordinary difficulty.

In connection with this point it must also be borne in mind that in British East Africa the natives are for the very large part, not soldiers, but agriculturists by nature; whereas German East Africa teems with natives who form as fine material for soldiers as any in the world. This point is always worth remembering since, because of it, while Germany held German East Africa, she was a potential menace to the whole continent.

Unity of command again was with the Germans to a striking degree. For on our side was ever command so divided ? Our main force working from East Africa contained troops from almost every portion of the globe, speaking different tongues, having different habits, eating different foods, fighting in different ways. From Nyasaland and Rhodesia, General Northey with his small force brilliantly fought his way into the enemy's country, for long not only not under our Commander-in-Chief, but not even administered by the War Office. From the west our most gallant Allies the Belgians pushed forward to Tabora, and later worked in direct co-operation into the very heart of the enemy's country. On the south there were the Portuguese.

The advantages which the Germans had over us in this matter were worth many thousands of rifles.

It is certainly undeniable that after the first eighteen months our combined force largely outnumbered our adversaries. Yet at his strongest Von Lettow probably mustered 25,000 to 30,000 rifles, all *fighting* troops. A not inconsiderable army on the basis that we, on our side, had to estimate that it took four to five soldiers to get one fighting man into the firing line.

It will naturally be assumed that at all events in the matter of equipment and arms we had the advantage, but until the very latest stages it may be doubted if this was so. Two incidents will illustrate this. During the latter part of 1916 a German prisoner, being taken past a spot where some of our artillery units, which shall be nameless, were parked, remarked, "the movable armament from the Ark, I should imagine!" And, indeed, his naval guns, his 42-in. howitzers, and quick-firing mountain guns were far ahead of anything in our possession. Again, late in 1917, a German doctor came in to demand back one of his medical panniers abandoned on the field. We returned it with reluctance, as it was a very fine set, the latest model in 1914.

However, in response to repeated and urgent indents and *hasteners*, new equipment for our own medical department was that moment arriving. It was far in advance of anything we had seen on our side, but was plainly marked 1906. I shall not soon forget the sneer on that doctor's face.

It is true that twice in the campaign the Germans were on short commons in the matter of small-arm ammunition, in spite of their enormous pre-war accumulation, but in each case, most unfortunately, a blockade runner relieved the situation. Later on, unfortunate captures prevented a shortage which would have appeared inevitable.

Again, the Germans worked throughout on interior lines and were able, for the most part, to choose the areas in which their resistance would be stiffest. Such spots were naturally where they would gain the fullest advantage from their knowledge of the country, and where the evil climate would exact the most murderous toll from our white and Indian troops. These considerations should, I think, be borne in mind by those who feel, as many must, that the cost in blood and money was altogether in excess of the results obtained. In any case it is to our credit that having put hand to the plough we did not turn back. It is for those who in the future will reap the benefit to see that the worthiest use is made of the vast country which the efforts of those who have fallen have placed in our hands.

The wild animal and bird life encountered throughout the campaign formed a most distinctive feature. This especially applies to the last stages, when the fighting in the south-east corner of the Colony was conducted in territory almost virgin to the naturalist. This applies equally to the insects both large and small, which in many cases were as unpleasant as they were intrusive. Captain Buchanan is well qualified to discourse on these subjects, and his observant notes are most instructive. Let us hope that some day he may find an opportunity of renewing his researches under happier circumstances.

In conclusion of these few remarks let me wish Captain Buchanan the utmost success in putting his book before the public. If only others read it with the same interest and enjoyment with which it has filled me, I can only think that the author's work will not have been in vain.

Cranworth

Preface

In accomplishing the conquest of German East Africa, many columns were put in the field. Those had their starting-points from the British East Africa frontier in the neighbourhood of Kilimanjaro Mountain, from Lake Victoria Nyanza, from the Belgian Congo, from Rhodesia, and latterly from the East Africa coast. To cover wide fronts of great extent of country, the forces from each of those bases advanced in their particular area in two, three, or more columns. This narrative deals directly with the operations of a single column, but, as operations throughout the columns were similar, it may be found, in part, to be generally descriptive of much that was experienced by all columns.

On actual operations in German East Africa—not including the operations on the frontier during 1915, nor the countless distances covered on patrol—our unit marched some 850 miles with the column, in the following stages: Kilimanjaro area, 194 miles; to the Central Railway, 335 miles; Morogoro-Rufiji area, 260 miles; and Lindi area (to date of my departure), 61 miles. Those distances are not direct to their objective as the crow flies, for they had often a zigzag course, and sometimes even doubled back to a fresh starting-point.

It has been my endeavour to include every detail of experience, and, in doing so, I trust that at some points I have not laid too much stress on the hardships of the campaign.

They were all in the day's work, and were taken as such, no matter how irksome they were. Of them General Smuts, in a dispatch of 27th October, 1916, said:

> Their work has been done under tropical conditions which not only produce bodily weariness and unfitness, but which create mental languor and depression, and finally appal the stoutest hearts. To march day by day, and week by week, through the African jungle or high grass, in which vision is limited? to a few yards, in which danger always lurks near, but seldom becomes visible, even when experienced, supplies a test to human nature often, in the long run, beyond the limits of human endurance.

Little reference has been made in the narrative to the number of our casualties, nor was that possible. A recent casualty statement—at the end of 1918—records the casualties of the East African Campaign as: 380 officers killed, 478 officers wounded, 8,724 other ranks killed, 7,276 other ranks wounded, 38 officers missing (including prisoners), and 929 other ranks missing (including prisoners) = 896 officers, 16,929 other ranks.

This is the only statement of casualties I have seen, and I give these figures with every reservation, doubting the aggregate and its completeness.

They will, however, suffice to show that there is a remarkable percentage of killed, and this may largely be put down to the closeness of the fighting, and that at times the attacking forces were advancing on entrenched positions without protection of any kind to themselves.

Angus Buchanan

CHAPTER 1

Outward Bound

It was raining in London. It had been raining all day, and for many days previous, and tonight the atmosphere of damp and greyness pervaded the very soul of the city outdoors.

Number Seven platform, at Waterloo Station, was crowded with troops and baggage, about to depart for service with the B.E.F. in East Africa. They had arrived at the station at 6 p.m. At 11 p.m. they were still there grouped about in talkative jollying clusters, apparently indifferent to the delay in entraining.

Everyone knows this type of crowd nowadays, but in this case, and as commonly with men garbed in identical uniform, no one could tell with any accuracy the remarkable variety of character of the men, or the extent of their notability, Joe Robson, who was standing apart—a quiet onlooker—thought: "It is almost a pity that the individual loses his individuality in the army and becomes a stranger in a strange crowd." What would that group of schoolboys say, and the inquisitive idle crowd in general, if they knew that here in the ranks, beneath the guise of homogeneous khaki, were gathered many men from all the world over? Men who had come to fight for their native land from Honolulu, Hong-Kong, China, Ceylon, Malay States, India, New Zealand, Australia, South and East Africa, Egypt, South America, Mexico, United States of America, and Canada? Men from the very outer edges of the world; in Ogilvie's words:

Lean men, brown men, men from overseas,
Men from all the outer world; shy and ill at ease.

Some were men who had taken part in Arctic exploration; others were of the Northwest Mounted Police and of the British South Africa Police; even a cowpuncher or two from under the flag of the U.S.A. were amongst this force of frontiersmen. And there were among them: good sorts, bad sorts, rich sorts, keen sorts, game sorts—all sorts!

Here also, holding the rank of subalterns, were some famous hunters, setting out again on adventure. F. C. Selous, the renowned big-game hunter and naturalist and explorer, was there, and Cherry Kearton, who, like his brother Richard, "shoots" with his camera and has specialised in photographing big game in Africa. Then there were George Outram and Martin Ryan, hailing from divergent corners of our colonies, who were reputed old hunters who knew, by long association, the vast hunting-grounds in Africa, as well as you or I, perhaps, know our grouse moor at home. And, lastly, at the head of all stood Colonel Driscoll, the leader of *Driscoll's Scouts* in the South African War.

Yes, there was a spirit of romance on Number Seven platform on this evening of April 1915. But, as is often the case with romance, it was obscure to the ordinary vision of the spectator, and but dully realised, if realised at all. So, for the most part, those troops remained commonplace, and passed from London, as thousands of other troops do, out to an unknown destination under cover of the night.

It was 2 o'clock next morning when, after long waiting, the train finally drew out of Waterloo. Between 11 p.m. and 1 a.m., by twos and threes, friends of the troops had taken their last farewells and departed, taking sadness with them, and leaving, here and there, a disconsolate soul behind.

How many touching, aye, last farewells have been witnessed by the soulless shed of that vast station since war began! How many brave souls have laughingly departed never to return!—their one great love their home, their Empire's honour.

The battalion's destination—the port of tailing was unknown, except to those in command, but in the early dawn of morning it became apparent to all, as we passed along the borders of Somerset and Dorset and on through Devon, that we were *en route* to Plymouth.

At 10 a.m. we drew up in Plymouth Docks, there to embark on H.M.T.S. *Neuralia* (Glasgow).

The day was spent in embarking the troops and baggage to their allocated stations on board ship; and in the depth of a pitch-black night, when all was ready, we cleared the docks and steamed slowly out of Plymouth Sound, in company with others of a convoy, and commenced our voyage *outward bound* to Africa.

There are times in all men's lives when they go through experiences that remain for ever remarkable, either because they are so new and unexpected, or because they contain so much of pain and hardship. The men new to travel—and there were a number of them—who embarked on the good ship *Neuralia* will remember, to the end of their days, their first experiences on board a troopship and their first voyage to the tropics; for it contained, for them, all the hardship of their new life of soldiering, and all the romance and pleasure of seeing a completely new and unexpected world.

Conversation on board ship dealt largely with contrasts. Old pictures were compared with new and, in most cases, within the mind of the intelligent individual each fresh experience brought new expression and wide awakening. Young men who short weeks before, and all their lives, had enjoyed all the comfort and ease of home life were now feeling the first rigour of army service.

Robson, an observant old soldier, heard much of his neighbours' little troubles. It was common to hear the warm, soft, white-sheeted bed at home ruefully recalled by the men, when rolled in coarse grey blankets on the hard deck, or, chrysalis-like, bound in hammocks slung from the ceiling in the impure atmosphere below. Also to hear, when men viewed their portions of bare, often ill-cooked rations, fond recollections of Sunday dinners at home, or a lucid description of a favourite dish. Personal comparisons those, which would have in time become odious had they not usually evoked laughter from some buoyant spirit, and the request to "Shut up, you old Funeral!"

It was much the same with everything of this new environment—the men's clothes, their boots, their fatigue work (deck-scrubbing, etc.), all were of a rougher nature than that to which they had been accustomed in pre-war life.

The process of securing and ensuring hardihood had begun, and, as time went on, the men, particularly the good ones, came to see the purpose of it and, generally, to laugh more than to *grouse* at their difficulties.

Were they not, after all, starting out on the greatest adventure of all—the stern pursuit of a perilous quest—and was not a rough life part of the setting to be expected and contested?

"Assuredly yes," thought Robson. "I who am an old traveller know it. Before you again see England you, who are *green hands*, will have seen and experienced what *roughing it* really is, and you will be the stronger men for it; you who live through."

While the change of personal surroundings was being discussed and searching out men's weaknesses, the *Neuralia* was proceeding daily on her way—over joying the men, in their idle hours, with the new scenes constantly presenting themselves, and stirring awake excited anticipation of the adventurous country to which they were going.

The ship's course—the war-time course—held south, well west of France and Spain and outside the Bay of Biscay. The first few days had been dull, for sea-sickness and strange quarters affect the best of spirits, but by the time the ship ran into Gibraltar, on the fourth day, everyone was about deck and cheerful.

No shore leave was granted at *Gib.*, nor was there any real time for it. The ship lay off *the Rock* only a few hours—the time required to take off, from launches, a few troops for Malta and some fresh vegetables. From the sea the towering Rock looked magnificent—grave, strong-featured, impressive. From the ship's side the eye could just discern the houses around the base of the promontory, clustered like molluscs on a rock, the white-bright dwellings of the inhabitants rising tier above tier from the water's edge to the sheer rock face a little distance inland from shore. A few fight sailing craft were dodging about in the foreground, out on their habitual occupation of the day, making pleasant pictures when they swept past with full white sail taut in the breeze. Alongside, a number of native row-boats, which had raced for the ship from shore as soon as it anchored, were doing thriving business in cigarettes, cigars, and tobacco, which gaily dressed Moors, and other low-caste tradesmen, were disposing of rapidly at their own figures to the improvident Tommies.

Dear old Gib., so proudly British, to many it was the entrance to the promised land of adventure, and the portal of farewell to things that are near and dear to home.

The ship sailed amid the gay raillery and cheers of Tommies to the barter-boats, but behind the laughter there lurked, perhaps, a tear, for this was the final, irrevocable, parting of the ways.

The good ship was now in the Mediterranean Sea—fast bidding good-bye to Europe, and with Northern Africa distantly in sight, at times, on our starboard beam.

It pleased many on board, at this stage, to get a hint of Africa's vastness. Here were they sighting the Continent on the fifth day out from England, and yet they knew that they must have about twenty days of travel, hugging her shores, before they could reach their destination on the East Coast of that same continent.

This set some of the more enterprising Tommies to establishing a *range card*, and, after questioning good-natured ship's

21

officers, they arrived at the information that our journey from Gib. to Mombasa was one of roughly some 6,000 miles.

This *range card* was:

	Miles
Gibraltar to Malta	1,200
Malta to Port Said	1,125
Port Said to Aden	1,675
Aden to Mombasa	1,950
Total	5,950

It was pleasant, now, forging ahead day after day, through sunny seas, neither storm-disturbed nor storm-delayed. Fair weather and placid sea, and the mellow wind of a southern spring—indeed we had found the Mediterranean in gracious mood. And under a clear sky is there another sea like that of the soft cobalt blue of the Mediterranean? It is not the commonplace sea, for it has lost all that is grey or blackish, and lives completely and wholly blue—blue as the overhead April sky; even more blue, more alluringly attractive.

On the morning of the eighth day the ship worked slowly into the snug but narrow harbour at Malta, while all along deck deeply interested troops conversed on the unfolding view of this quaint and foreign port, dressed for the business of war and bristling with grim fortifications.

British and French warships lay in harbour, and merchant vessels of all kinds—suggestive of the great activities of war in this quarter of the world, for here routes touched to the war zones of Egypt, Gallipoli, Mesopotamia, India, and Africa.

Here, as at Gibraltar, the boat hawking tobacco vendors arrived alongside from shore in their small craft, plying clamorous trade with the good-natured troops, until the arrival of the coal barges put them to flight.

The ship coaled all day and late into night; a process conducted by swarms of gibbering ill-thriven Maltese natives, meagrely garbed in ragged loin-cloths, who filed, endlessly, up plank gangways from the barges to the coal bunkers in the ship's side, each with his loaded wicker basket hoisted shoulder high.

Coaling is a filthy business. Before evening, despite awnings and closed port-holes, the fine coal-dust had sought its way into every conceivable corner of the ship, to be roundly abused and accused by a thousand discomforted Tommies. None were sorry to get it over, and all rejoiced when, the following morning, the ship hove anchor and took again to the clean-winded open sea.

Before departing, at early dawn, it was a strange sight to see row-boats from shore dredging the shallow harbour, with small bag nets, for the oddments of coal which had fallen overboard during the process of coaling—patient labour for a mere pittance of reward that forcibly suggested the value of fuel to the low-caste natives of the island.

Fair weather continued, and the next few days were as pleasant and generous of speed as those preceding our arrival at Malta. A noteworthy occurrence was the northern-bound migration of bird life which was encountered on the 19th and 20th of April. Many swallows and doves were seen and a few yellow wagtails, while a white-throat and a screech owl were picked up on deck. At the time most migration was observed the ship was about in a longitudinal line with the island of Crete.

On the morning of the twelfth day the ship arrived at Port Said, at the entrance of the Suez Canal, and anchored for a few hours—not long enough to go ashore and get any real first impression of the place. But it marked an important stage in the voyage; and the colonial, somewhat oriental, appearance of the town on the west shore of the canal entrance, close to which the ship had anchored, was predictive of things Egyptian, and of the weird beauty and strangeness of the Land of Deserts.

Leaving Port Said, the Suez Canal was entered, and slowly the ship proceeded on her course up the narrow fairway;

but not before sand-bags had been stacked on the bridge for protection from enemy sniping, for we were now in a theatre of war.

On entering the canal, which, between its low banks, is straight and of apparent width of a city thoroughfare, the first view, at this season, is of mud flats and shallow sheets of water, like flooded fen country; colourless of green, except for a few isolated tufts of grass or dwarfed shrub.

Soon this changes to the dry level plain of sand desert, endless as far as eye can see on land, and featureless in geographical outline if one seeks profile or form. There were many outposts stationed along the canal, safeguarding it from Turkish enemy who longed to wreak destruction on it. And they made picturesque scenes, those outposts on the desert, with their chalk-white groups of clustered conical tents, standing prominent in the unbroken desolation of pale wastes of sand. On the outskirts of camp were a few patient camels and some soldiers—helmeted British Tommies or turbaned Indians—all sharply outlined in firm silhouette, since they were darker in colour than the dead flat background.

By evening the ship was well up the canal, and the scene was very beautiful and impressive then. Far as the eye could see on either side were deep desolate stretches of limitless desert, unbroken by the slightest undulation. Overhead, the sky was soft and peculiar; singularly wistful and hazed and unlike any sky one sees at home, while a brilliant rainbow, foreboding, perhaps, a light shower of rain, lit up and went out low on the north-east horizon, away, apparently, at the uttermost edges of the world, where sand and sky merged almost without any visible line.

It was strange brooding country, and it infused a vein of solemnity into the atmosphere, for it held a suggestion that it had something to say, could it but give utterance, as an unexpressed thought may do which lies dormant for unknown ages through the long, long life of mankind.

At daybreak the ship arrived at Port Suez, having completed the passage through the canal during the night. Here ammunition was taken on board before proceeding onward a few hours later.

Suez was left with regret. Many were sorry to go to sea from a land so attractively picturesque and so full of indefinite mystery.

And in after days it was men's habit to look back on this one brief glimpse of Egypt and recall it as the most novel and memorable picture of the many which unfolded before their eyes on their voyage to Africa. The fast-moving ship was now sailing the Red Sea, and we were experiencing that for which it is famed—excessive heat. Damp, cold, and wintry it had been in England when the troops had sailed, and men had cursed the weather roundly, as soldiers will, but now, lolling listlessly about deck, victims of oppressive heat, they would fain have recalled a little of that northern temperature for the benefit of bodily comfort. However, the heat brought about one good service, for it caused the "powers that be" to issue orders for all ranks to hand in their home service kit to Stores and be supplied with the light tropical khaki drill outfit customarily worn in hot climates.

The troops were now settled to the routine of ship-board, and in leisure hours even the novelties of sea and new scenes became less astonishing the more they grew familiar with them.

The days in the Red Sea passed without particular incident. The weather remained phenomenally fine, and the sea charmingly clear and blue—almost as blue as that of the Mediterranean. Large numbers of flying fish were seen soon after leaving Port Suez; the first of their kind to be observed. With their transparent wings and long bodies they looked like magnified dragonflies in their short flights over the water.

About this time the shortening of the hours of daylight was noticeable. On the 26th of April dawn was at 5 a.m. and dusk at 6.45 p.m. The North Pole Star, too, was now low on

25

the horizon, as the ship drew farther and farther away from the northern hemisphere, and nearer to the Equator.

On the 17th day land was in sight on both bows. Strange land; of pronounced geographical change in the formation of the prominent mountains. They were not generally round and rolling and soft as the hills at home, but flat-topped, and severe as a cliff-head at their summit, their steep-rearing slopes terminating abruptly in a definite horizontal line. The whole was apparently rock and boulder, barren of any covering of foliage.

The sight of land was a forewarning of approach to Aden, and late at night, some hours after dark, anchor was dropped outside the harbour.

There was little sleep for anyone on board at Aden, unless you had cast-iron nerves and hearing, for coaling was started almost immediately the ship anchored, and continued throughout the night. The uproar of a thousand puny jabbering lascars, and the run of the coal down the chutes, made merry music for devils' ears, but not for sleepless Tommies.

Next morning, before sailing, Aden was viewed from the ship's side, but it was too far to land to glean much. The settlement was at the base of towering ragged mountains and, judging by the gathering of houses close to the shore front, it was apparently a small place, and principally a military station.

Here, for the first time, numbers of that well-known camp thief, the Egyptian kite, were seen gathering their food by robbing the defenceless gulls of the meat scraps that they picked up overboard.

At 10.30 a.m. Aden was left behind. It was the final port *en route,* and the ship steamed down the Gulf against a light headwind on the last lap of the voyage. She was soon well out to sea, and land was not sighted again until, six days later, her destination was approached. The third day out from Aden, in dead calm weather in the Indian Ocean, the best run of the voyage was recorded—337 miles.

Otherwise the final days were uneventful, except that there

was a good deal of bustle and confusion in preparation to land. Arms and ammunition were issued, equipment fitted, and everything got in readiness for the journey up country to the frontier, which was to be immediately undertaken on arrival in port.

On the morning of the 4th of May the battalion landed at Mombasa—-twenty-four days after our departure from Plymouth.

The bugle sounded *réveillé* at 5 a.m.—one hour earlier than usual; and while all were dressing, low-lying shore came into sight, rich with abundant tropical tree growth, and green, for it was the rainy season and leaf was new. A little later the ship anchored in the harbour of Kilindini, and, in due course, commenced the disembarkation of troops and stores into barges, and thence to the landings on shore. It was late evening ere the labours of transportation had ceased and all were landed and entrained, ready to proceed up country in the narrow, antiquated, wood-seated carriages of which the train was composed.

There had been no time for cooking, and everyone was hungry, for the last meal had been at 12 noon on the previous day. However, some hours after commencing the train journey, the train was stopped at a small wayside station about midnight, and hot tea and rations were served to the famishing troops. In after days all knew much more about going hungry—not for a day, but for many days—but, looking back now, it was strange that the very first experience in Africa was one of short rations and lean *interiors*.

Thus an imperial unit had come to East Africa; to join Indian and Native African forces already holding the frontier against the enemy in German East Africa.

CHAPTER 2

Frontier Life

Routine in the early days of war, in the camps on the frontier of British East Africa in 1915, was like unto a watch-dog's duties.

The Uganda Railway, running parallel to the boundary from Mombasa, on the East Coast, to Kisumu, on Lake Victoria Nyanza, had to be vigorously protected from raiding parties; and a force larger than our own had to be held at bay until a sufficient army could be sent out to take the field and the offensive.

Small encampments, manned with a handful of daring, miscellaneous soldiers, had sprung into being all along the frontier.

Every station along the boundary was alert and aware of the presence of enemy; and frequent were the alarms and skirmishes.

Amongst thorn-bush, in dreary landscape of consistent sameness, those stations were everywhere hidden—a mere gathering of small tents, within limited enclosures built up of sharp-spiked, tangled, thorn-tree branches. These enclosures were called *bomas*, and were, against an enemy surprise, as complete a protection as barbed wire. Water, always the chief concern of existence in Africa, was usually in the neighbourhood of those encampments. Sometimes, if the camp was a main station, water was brought by pipe line from the hills; but most often, the supply for a small camp was that of the adjacent muddy *water hole*. They were those stagnant pools of water so often spoken of by travellers who have written of interior Africa and know her thirst. Those pools of water—a single pool in a swampy bed or in a barren river bottom—are of uncertain quality and of uncertain supply. It was usual to place a guard over such scanty supply, and order a very bare ration to be served to each individual each day.

Patrols were the chief concern of those bush encampments. They were unceasingly active, daily, nightly, moving out into the vague, half-unmapped country, to cover many miles in quest of enemy patrols or raiding parties.

Those patrols seldom covered less than ten miles a day, more often twenty miles; while occasionally long distances were covered that necessitated a party being out from three to six days.

In this manner the frontier was kept fairly clear of enemy; especially in the neighbourhood of the camps. The grass was tall, and the bush, in places, very heavy, so that ambush and surprise encounters were not infrequent. On those occasions casualties were, sometimes, on both sides heavy; but usually it was the side which laid the ambush which scored most heavily. To illustrate this: on one occasion, on the 4th of September, 1915, at Maktau, a party of our M.I. was ambushed and rather badly cut up by the enemy. The casualties in killed were eleven Europeans and three Indians. During this encounter a young British officer named Dartnell won the V.C. for refusing to surrender to the enemy, and fighting right out to a finish against great odds. Ten days later this same enemy company was ambushed by our forces and completely routed, leaving thirty dead Askaris and one German officer on the battle-ground.

On the whole it was this sort of ding-dong fighting all along, with the British forces holding the stronger hand. Patrols were constantly expectant of an engagement of some description, and many became very expert bushmen as months of this type of fighting went on.

On the *19th June,* 1915, four hundred of our unit found themselves de-training at Kisumu, on Lake Victoria Nyanza, after a long train journey which had lasted one day and one night. On the low shore of the lake edge they camped, near to the wharf and half-roofed freight sheds, while other detachments came in on the railway and joined the force. During the day, there were concentrated here, beside us, detachments of 29th Punjabis, King's African Rifles, Loyal North Lancashires; and 28th Mountain Battery, with their array of fine looking Sepoys, and sturdy, well-groomed, well-fed mules.

By noon on the following day, which was a Sunday, everyone had been packed on to the small lake steamship craft which lay at the wharf in readiness, and the expedition sailed thenceforth, out through the Kavirondo Gulf into the great lake.

The ships had been filled to their utmost capacity, above deck and below, and it was a motley crowd that occupied every yard of deck space, while pack-mules and store cattle stood roped to the ship's rails on the upper deck. Forward, each vessel had a gun mounted, and a space roped off and cleared for action.

Thus we sailed from Kisumu to raid the town of Bukoba on the 22nd and 23rd June; a prosperous trade town within the German colony, on the south-west shores of the lake, which was the base of enemy activities against the Uganda Frontier in the vicinity of the Kagera River, and which contained a powerful wireless plant, by which the enemy were able to obtain, and send, important communications.

All night, and all the next day, we sailed the great lake, Victoria Nyanza, and we had been some thirty hours on board when, at sundown on the second day, we drew near to the enemy's territory and slowed down, awaiting the fall of darkness.

It was thought to effect a night landing and make a surprise attack on the town, and plans were all prepared for this. In this connection three privates were voluntarily selected for a novel undertaking: it was arranged that an Australian bush-man, a Canadian from the Yukon, and self (I was then a private) were to go ahead at landing and try to overpower, and kill if necessary, a certain sentry whose post was known to our command. But all plans were changed in the end, for, about midnight, when our lightless phantom ships were drawing in to Bukoba, wakeful watchers on a high island, that lay out in the bay before the town, detected our approach in the light of the half-full moon, and five great rockets shot in warning into the sky. The alarm was out! Soldiers in the town would be rushing to arms and our landing on the beach would now be in the face of enemy waiting to receive us. Thus, plans were changed, and the ships drew away from shore, beyond the vision of the enemy, and stood to, waiting for dawn.

When dawn approached we again moved toward land. A force was to threaten a landing away south of the town, while the main forces drew in behind a long promontory north of Bukoba Bay.

Close on dawn our ship dropped anchor and boats were lowered; and, one by one, they were filled with troops, and left the ship's side for shore; while the ship trembled from stem to stern beneath the shock of her gun-fire, which was now rapidly shelling the heights before us, and the hidden positions beyond. Beneath the steep hill-face of the promontory each boat ran aground on the beach, and the troops scrambled overboard and waded ashore.

It was breaking daylight when we began riling up the steep mountain-side, which was cliff-like in places, and the climb to the top proved a stiff one, of close on a mile in distance, and very breathless were we when the summit was reached, while we judged it our great good fortune that this awkward ground had been covered unopposed by enemy. Advancing across the summit, south toward Bukoba, some resistance was encountered there in the banana plantations and forest, but the real fighting did not begin until we reached the southern slopes and looked out on the town of Bukoba, some two miles distant, situated on low land that swept back from the shores of the lake to the foot of the hills, and over the intervening bouldered, rocky hill country, and on to the commanding heights, above the town, on the west and south. It was then that serious fighting began, and all day—while the ships shelled from the lake—we fought in attack against the enemy, who, to begin with, held out amongst the rocks and clumps of trees in the broken hills before us, and who, latterly, defended the commanding hills north-west of the town.

It was real guerilla warfare. From rock to rock one could see men dodge, while puffs of smoke puffed in and out from behind scores of rocks, and from many a tree-clump bottom. The enemy were here using the old ·450 rifle and black powder and lead bullets, hence the prominence of the smoke-puffs. On the whole front all was visible, even the enemy's single piece of artillery, which was plainly seen in position by the river-side in the low flat ground north of the town, and which the mountain battery guns in a short time knocked out of action, before turning their attention to the enemy machine-guns, which were not so easy to deal with.

In the afternoon we worked down the last of the hill-slopes under constant fire of our foes, and, toward evening, gathering our tired limbs under us, a charge was ordered. Across an open meadow we doubled, cheering lustily; through swamp and river, almost neck-high in water, and, finally, up the hill-side opposite, and on to the lower hill-top of the enemy's coveted position commanding the town; there to lie, panting breathlessly, picking off the fleeing enemy that we could see dodging among the rocks in endeavour to reach the higher hill, across a ravine and to the west of us.

Meantime the Loyal North Lancashires, who had made a wide flank movement, were advancing in on the higher hill from the west; and ere darkness set in we were in full possession of the chief positions.

Had there been more daylight, it is possible that we should

have taken the town this day, for the enemy were on the run; but darkness overtook us, and night gave the enemy opportunity to reorganise.

We camped for the night on the hill, chilled, and blanketless, and foodless; for no supplies followed us as it was a short undertaking. In the early part of the night, the force which had made a demonstration to the south of the town were landed on the beach near to us, and joined our force.

At daylight a fighting line was formed across the flats, from the hills to the lake; and an advance began toward the town in face of steady rifle and machine-gun fire. The river we had crossed yesterday had swung southward and ran parallel with the lake, and here again proved an obstacle, and many of us got thoroughly wet crossing and recrossing it. Also, in the morning, in the heat of the early fighting, a thunderstorm burst and heavy rains fell, while we lay in the grass drenched to the skin for an hour or two, and rifle locks choked with sand and moisture. For a time firing ceased on both sides; to resume again as it cleared. Bit by bit, we pushed on across the flat, to be held up for a time before the entrance to the town; and then, breaking the opposition down, to enter the town without further resistance on the heels of the fleeing foe.

But there we did not stop, for our unit passed on through the town—which had a beautiful broad main road parallel to the lake front, and many fine Colonial residences within flower-decked, shaded grounds—and occupied the high hill-summit on the south, while, in the town, the great power-house containing the wireless plant, and the fort, and all ammunition and stores, were blown up and destroyed by our engineers.

Late in the afternoon we evacuated the hills and came down through banana plantations on to the road and into the town; there to witness the impressive burial of our fallen comrades near to the central square.

At sundown re-embarkation commenced, and at daylight the following day the ships drew out from Bukoba pier, and lay to, waiting until the outlying pickets were gathered in. When they put out from shore and were taken aboard, we steamed away northward to get back within our frontier, while most men lay down anywhere and slept, for there had been little rest since we had landed three days ago.

On the 26th June we were again in Kisumu, and were given a joyous reception by the natives, who showed extraordinary interest in the affair.

Three days later we were back in camp—back to the bush, and the routine of frontier patrols.

To give some little idea of the ordinary days of life in a frontier encampment the following notes may serve:

Maktau, 20th Aug., 1915—Fortifying camp, taken over yesterday. All day on trench construction. Gangs of our fellows working well and cheerfully. Hearty jokes among themselves constantly brace them against their trying labours in the excessive heat. Patrol attacked near camp this morning by enemy party trying to mine the railway. One private killed, three wounded. The enemy scattered and cleared off as soon as the first surprise shots were over. They attacked from hiding cover in the bush, whence they had viewed the approach of our patrol down the bare straight line of the single-track railway.

Maktau, 21st Aug., 1915—On trench work all day, same as yesterday. Dust-begrimed and filthy. Hope for opportunity to wash and change to-morrow. Last night an Indian sentry was shot by enemy who crept up to the camp entrance in the darkness.

Maktau, 22nd Aug., Sunday—Trench work in early morning and again in forenoon; then *knocked off* all hands for Sunday relaxation. Early this morning enemy again on Voi railway near here. This time they succeeded in laying mines which blew up the line and derailed an incoming train. Enemy got clear away.

Maktau, 23rd Aug., 1915—Railway line repaired and open

34

to traffic this morning. On outpost last night on *kopje* below Signal Hill. Nothing untoward occurred, though this picket had been twice attacked lately. Strong S.W. monsoon blowing: bitterly cold for sentries on windward front of *kopje*. Damp mist driving over the level bushland below us, obscuring everything in the early morning.

Silent dawn, except for the strident cry of guinea-fowl, spur-fowl, and horn-bills; and the lesser *cheepings* of awakening songbirds that mouse-like stirred amongst the surrounding foliage. Picket relieved at 9 a.m. It was dark at 6.15 p.m. and day dawned at 5.30 a.m. Sunrise three-quarters of an hour later.

Maktau, 28th Aug., 1915—Out on patrol all day over country west of camp. Party, ten whites and two natives. Uneventful day—no enemy sighted or tracked. Three rhinoceros encountered at close quarters; one being a very large one with splendid forehead horns. All were allowed to go their way unmolested, since they showed no inclination to charge, and pleasure shooting was not permissible in enemy country.

Maktau, 3rd Sept., 1915—Out on reconnaissance, to position enemy holding about eight miles west of our camp. Moving quietly through bush—our party two whites and two porters.

On outward journey ran across a rhinoceros, who charged on hearing stick break underfoot; but he stopped about ten yards short, when he then got our wind, and cleared off rapidly with a quick turn and snort, apparently afraid of us. Self and companion, at the sound of the rushing crash of the charge, had backed behind stoutish trees, with rifles ready, but the natives, in an incredibly short moment, had squirmed frantically into the bushes overhead. They were fully frightened, poor wretches—but they were low-caste porters.

Observations were made of enemy camp while lying close to position in evening and early part of night. Later, slept under a tree in the bush. Night bitterly cold; dozed intermittently, but keeping a wakeful uneasy eye for the most part. Idly watching the stars when awake. The Southern Cross set about 9.30 p.m. and the pointers about midnight.

Saw many eland on return journey, beautiful beasts. In shape and solid form they are at a distance like Jersey cattle in an English park. Also saw one lion, three jackals, some herds of Grant's gazelle, and about a dozen mongoose.

On reaching camp heard of M.I. engagement, already mentioned, from which our men had just returned. On our travels we had almost been over the ground on which the engagement took place, yet in the maze of bush and tall grass we had seen nothing. It is very difficult, for those who have not seen the country, to conceive how terribly possible secretive work is in this virgin bush-land, where vegetation grows luxuriant and rank in vast uninhabited areas. It is not the enemy in themselves that are the difficult foe to conquer; it is the bush that hampers everything, and hides almost all of the evil planned against us. The unpleasant game, though it is a game on a much larger scale, is like hunting a snake in the long grass. And who was ever sure of trapping a snake unless he was come upon unawares, and a complete ring formed around his chosen cover? Even then, notwithstanding the great care with which the cordon may close in, the snake may escape through an unguarded yard of grass, just as a patrol, or an army, if it has sharp eyes everywhere, may escape, under cover of the screening bush, through the narrowest of openings and be gone and hopelessly lost in a single night.

Maktau, 1st Oct., 1915—Today an aeroplane made an ascent from camp. This is the first flight made here, and the African natives were spell-bound in amazement at sight of the wonderful machine and its graceful flying. At once they termed it *Ndege* (the Swahili for bird), and thereafter they always called aeroplanes by that name. 'Planes should prove of immense value to us out here now that they have been landed in the   country. The Germans have no machines, and are very unlikely to succeed in securing any, since they are isolated from the outer world and the open seas.

Tieta Hills, 26th Dec, 1915—After holding the ranks of private, lance-corporal, corporal, and lance-sergeant, it has been my fortune to receive my commission. I leave the ranks with regret, for it has, on the whole, been a gay, care-free, rough-and-tumble experience, and one which teaches that among all types "a man's a man for a' that," and that there are few who have not their finer feelings beneath any kind of veneer.

At 9.30 p.m. moved out to watch railway, at a point five miles from camp, hoping to catch mine-layers. Dark night; starlit sky, but no moon. Sentries on outskirts of camp spoken to, and passed. Party wearing moccasins, boots on hard road or in dry bush very noisy. Alert to catch the slightest sound, hearing being more important than sight in the darkness.

About 11 p.m. held up by rhinoceros moving about on left of road, breaking undergrowth and branches close ahead. Could not see whether he meant to charge or not, and there was a moment's suspense on that account, but eventually he moved off quietly. Later, at first railway crossing over road, below a great dark mango tree on the river-side, the leading scout caught a glint of the small, red glow of a dying fire. We halted and waited, but no sound was audible, though a man's breathing could have almost been heard in the calm stillness. On venturing forward, a deserted fire, almost out, was found. Whoever lit it had used it and gone, but they had left a mark that would arouse suspicion. Such signs of the enemy's presence were constantly being found. The moon rose at 10.30. Everything clear then, and our forms, moving stealthily along at wide intervals, showed dark on the dust-white road. Reached point on road overlooking railway about midnight and lay down in bush, each of the four comprising the party in turn keeping watch to detect any movement of enemy.

Night passed, quietly, stirred only by African sounds. Among the high trees on the river-bank, beyond the railway, monkeys yelled occasionally and snapped off dry branches as they swung from limb to limb. A solitary owl hoo-hooed away out in the distant darkness, and once or twice the weird clatter-ratchet of a horn-bill, wakeful in the moonlight, like a barn-door fowl, broke the stillness. Sometimes, too, an animal of prey would betray its presence and its prowling: the deep blood-curdling howl of the hyena and the dog-like bark of the jackal at times awoke the silence, for one or two brief moments, ere, phantom-like, they were swallowed in the dark, fathomless pit of night, and lost on their onward trail.

At daybreak, white morning mists came down over the bush-land and obscured everything; soon they rose again and cleared. Back from the roadside, in the bush, we made a small fire and warmed and cheered ourselves with a hot cup of tea. Later we returned pleasantly to camp, having joined in with the railway patrol, which came out along the line at daybreak some fifty strong.

Namanga, 27th Feb., 1916—A small reconnaissance patrol climbed the densely bush-forested slope of Ol Doinyo Orok mountain today. Mountain-sides overcrowded with trees, cactus, and undergrowth, in tropical uncultivated confusion. Contrary to the usual in country of this nature, no roller-like game paths of the ponderous rhinoceros could be found breaking a way to the higher ground. The ascent was therefore begun up a small river-course, in a delightfully picturesque ravine down which trickled and murmured a stream of running water. Progress was made slowly up this water-course, for the way was continually obstructed by huge granite boulders, and cliff-like falls which were surmounted only by the aid of a rope. By stiff climbing we completed about half the ascent, and were then confronted with impassable cliffs over which scanty water trickled. The patrol then branched off the course of the stream, and attempted to find easier passage through the forest above the ravine on the right. This forest, however, proved desperately difficult to penetrate, compelling us to continual stooping, and forcing of way, through cruel barriers of jagged, tearing thorn. Here, too, the ascent was very steep, and, at times, detours had to be made to avoid an unclimbable cliff face. Defeat was unpalatable; otherwise we must early on have given up the undertaking. As it was, we stuck grimly to our task, and finally reached the summit at 4.30 p.m.

On our ascent on the east bank of the river, a cave had been found which, by reason of newly cut sticks and an old fire, had evidently been used by enemy scouts, at the time of our advance into this area, a few days previously. Otherwise, the mountain held no signs of recent occupation.

After resting a short time, and exploring the plateau on the summit, the descent was commenced. All might have gone well, but darkness came down before we were half-way out of the bush, and then our troubles really began. It was impossible to see more than a yard before one, and thorn and boulders and pitfalls played havoc with faces and limbs, as downward we clambered laboriously in the inky darkness. It was, at one time, proposed, in despair, to give up, and to camp where we were without blankets, but at that time some one made the inspired suggestion to use lighted faggots. This idea was carried into force, and by the aid of their uncertain light we were able to grapple with, and partly avoid, the barriers of cruel fanged bush, and at last managed to extricate ourselves from the deep forest of shapeless, sightless jungle. But not until the entire patrol was torn and bleeding and sore, and completely, almost hopelessly, tired out. They were sadder and wiser men who wearily dragged into camp long after midnight, avowing everlasting denunciation on African jungle.

Nevertheless expeditions of this kind were commonplace enough to scouts who endeavoured to understand almost every landmark on our border that might harbour the enemy. Sometimes they were fruitless expeditions, sometimes they were the means of obtaining valuable information.

For the greater part of the year those frontier operations were carried on in the excessively hot, unchangeable climate of tropical Africa. Through the intensive heat of the piercing overhead sun, the routine work went on day after day, and month after month. Not until December was there change, and then there was a period of heavy torrential rains. But ere the month was out they had ceased again, and the rich green foliage of the acacias, which had sprung in a day to life, had begun to fade and lose their freshness; so soon does the blazing sun dry up the abundant rainfall, and scorch the very earth.

Locusts, and their following of storks, are heralds of the rains, and near to that season great clouds of them were seen. Remarkable swarms of locusts were witnessed on the 25th November and 5th December, 1915, and again on 21st February, 1916. Great clouds of them, darkening the very sky in their tens of millions, drifted down wind slowly, in a south-westerly direction, over camp on those dates; and above them, on the last occasion, high in the sky, followed a very large flight of black and white storks, sailing along, with the ease of a floating feather, with wing-still, wind-poised motion, apparently planing on the banking of the air; and now and then checking their onward flight, to swing slowly and gracefully in a circle, as if to hesitate and examine the ground far underneath them.

At the time of the rains, too, fresh snow fell on Mount Kilimanjaro, the highest mountain in Africa, with the elevation of over 19,700 feet. In 1915 the first fresh snowfall was on 25th November, and on the morning of that day a new white coat of snow mantled the peaks of Kibo and Mawensi, and well down their slopes.

Mount Kibo.   Mount Mawensi.

KILIMANJARO FROM SOUTH-WEST : 19,700 FEET.

A native once told me that if he could climb to the far-off glistening snows, he would find rupees. And he seemed seriously to believe that the snows, which glinted silver-like in the sun, were unattainable wealth.

On the frontier, when not scouting, or on patrol, or on picket, it sometimes fell to our lot to have a day in camp.

In camp, *réveillé* was at 5.30 a.m.—just about daybreak. The able men then dressed, and, outside their tents, shook out their dust and insect-ridden blankets, in which they had slept on the bare hard ground. The lazy, and the seedy, and the really sick men, slept on fitfully until the last possible moment before the "Fall In," at 6.30 a.m.; then reluctantly to turn out in cheerless spirit.

On early morning parade "the roll" was first called. The sick were then excused from duty, and the remainder marched off with shovels and picks and axes to dig trenches and construct overhead shell-shelters, wherever the fortifications of our encampment required strengthening.

Such mornings passed quickly, and work went ahead, for, in the cool of the rising day, the labours were not unpleasant. Most men made light of their morning's work, and enjoyed getting up a keen healthy appetite ere the "Fall Out" for 8 o'clock breakfast.

Breakfast consisted generally of a measured ration of bread, cheese, and tea: sometimes bacon replaced the cheese, sometimes jam.

The second morning parade fell in at 9 a.m., and again the men in camp were sent on to the fortifications. But now work was carried on in the heat of the tropic sun, for a soldier's duties are at any hour of the day or night, and in any weather, in any hemisphere. They laboured on in the heat, swearing and joking (I think a soldier will joke, aye, even in H———) and perspiring, and with faces   and clothes smothered in the fine red lava sand, which was raised by the labouring picks and shovels, or which incessantly wafted downwind in gusts off the bare compound of the encampment. But, nevertheless, the work went forward, for it had to go, and defences became duly more and more impregnable. About noon the working party fell out for lunch, which consisted of a ration of bread, jam, and tea.

Lunch over, the men rested until 4.30 p.m. Some fitfully slept under stifling hot canvas, others washed clothes down by the trough, or bathed themselves with water from a bucket, standing naked in the open; while still others gambled, mildly, over halfpenny nap and threepenny bridge.

The afternoon parade fell in at 4.30 p.m. and worked as before on trenches for another hour and a half. It was then time to "Fall Out" for dinner.

Dinner consisted *always,* of badly cooked stew, an unchanging dish which became deadly monotonous, and which, in time, many men could not touch, their palate revolted so strongly against the unseasoned, uninviting mixture.

I have particularly mentioned food, because, even when rations were full—and they were often not—our soldiers were nearly always troubled with that subject throughout the East Africa Campaign. It is wonderful what men, living outdoors, can subsist on, but, at the same time, I will never believe that the cut-and-dry army ration, as served in Africa, is sufficient for men carrying on arduous operations in an intensely tropical climate. All units experienced a tremendous amount of sickness, and I am certain, in my own mind—and many others agree with me—that at least half of the sickness was caused, directly or indirectly, from lack of full and proper nourishment for a prolonged period. Transport difficulties, and the greater wars in Europe, no doubt had a strong guiding influence with the commissariat; and for such, allowances must be made. I have but little inclination to raise the subject now, for the roughness of war is always to be expected and borne, but for the future it is well to write down the harsh experiences of the past so that others, in like undertakings, may gain an insight into such things, and prepare for them, or seek to obtain a reconstruction. Food was a big question in Africa, and, if such a campaign should be called for again in any far-off country, administrators would do well to give serious thought to a serious subject that might well in the end save the nation both life and expenditure.

On the frontier, men had very few means of adding to their rations. Parcels from home, in many cases, found them most of the luxuries they ever enjoyed. Again, at some places a venturous Goanese trader set up small wood-framed shack-stores, and dispensed to the troops a few odds and ends in very limited quantities. The chief luxuries (?) which the men sought I give below, and a comparison in African and English prices:

	Trader's Price		English Price, 1915	
	S.	D.	S.	D.
TEA, PER LB	2	6½	1	10
SUGAR, PER LB	0	6½	0	1½
BUTTER, PER LB	1	4	1	2
MILK, CONDENSED	0	11	0	6½
WORCESTER SAUCE	2	0	0	9
SOAP, PER LB	0	10½	0	3½
CIGARETTES, KING STORK, PER 10	0	2	—	—

On those groceries, or such-like, every penny of a man's pay was often spent the day he received it. Whenever the trader received a fresh lot of goods the news would fly about camp, and, as soon as nightfall came and liberated the soldiers from duty, he would be besieged by toil-worn troops hungry for luxuries, and speedily everything in demand would be sold out.

In one other way was it sometimes possible to obtain a change of diet: that was by game shooting. A good many buck, wart-hog, guinea-fowl, and partridges found their way into camp at one time or other, and furnished a few fortunate ones with a very welcome addition to the routine fare.

One of the first hunting outings which I experienced was with Capt. W., Lieut. F. C. Selous, and the *Doc*, when I accompanied them on a trek to make a sketch of certain country they were going into. We were at this time camped in the open upland bush near Kajiado. Mounted on mules we had travelled overnight to a selected camp. Selous—fine sportsman that he was—was as keen as ever on a hunt, and the party were merry as sandboys.

Next morning all were astir at daylight. Before breakfast some spur-fowl were shot close to the near-by waterhole, and fried for the meal. They were delicious eating. After breakfast the mules were saddled and mounted, and we rode onward. In the forenoon we sighted one lion—which escaped under cover of a thickly bushed valley—two warthog, three water-buck, a few hartebeests and impala, and many giraffe. Selous had an unsuccessful shot at an impala, but, otherwise, the game were allowed to go unmolested, as all were wild and no exceptionally good heads were singled out. We made the noon halt in rolling, somewhat open bush country and haltered the mules, to picket them there. After lunching the party went in divergent directions on foot. Capt. W. and self proceeded to the highest hill-crest in the neighbourhood, and I there settled for the afternoon to pencil a panoramic sketch of the country before me. Capt. W. then left me. Later I learned he had, on his return tramp to camp, shot a hartebeest for meat. But game proved very wary. Selous and the *Doc.* returned without securing a single head, though they had seen impala, eland, giraffe, and a rhinoceros. Masai natives were grazing many cattle in this area at the time of our visit, and the game were evidently kept moving and wild by constant disturbance of the cattle and their cattle-herds. At any rate, as far as game heads, and meat, were concerned, it was not a successful outing. But it was all very enjoyable and a holiday from soldiering. To me it was a memorable outing because it recalls to mind one of my first meetings with Selous. It was the first of many meetings, for, in after days, we joined in many a successful hunt, the old hunter and the young attracted together by a mutual enthusiasm for nature and the open road.

These, above, are a few notebook entries. It will be seen that a soldier's life in 1915 was not without variety and adventure in a theatre of war of which the outer world, in those days, heard very little. Yet it was the beginning of a great undertaking which, in its turn, has been overshadowed, almost overlooked, on account of the gigantic world-war raging in Europe, and resounding on England's doorstep.

Towards the end of 1915 rumours were prevalent that strong South African forces were to arrive in the country.

About the same time the Germans, who apparently had information of our movements, increased their activities on the border from Voi to Kilindini. Perhaps their biggest effort at interference was when a strong force of Germans occupied the prominent hill position of Kasigau and threatened the Uganda Railway from the S.E. of Voi. Obviously, if they could break on to our only up-country railway and line of communication, at such a time, they had much to gain. However, in this they were forestalled. Forces were sent to oppose them in their mountain stronghold, on the heels of their arrival, and eventually they were forced to evacuate without accomplishing anything.

At this period signs were not wanting of the coming of forces. Around the old camps extensive spaces were cleared of bush in readiness for camping grounds. Supplies of all kinds arrived daily, by train or by wagon transport, and were stacked in huge piles in the open. Everywhere, in the frontier camps, could be seen added activities and increased optimism.

For two months this sort of thing had been going on, until one fine day—the 16th of January, 1916—the first large contingent of South African troops passed through Voi, and detrained at Maktau. The critical period was over; here was compensation at last for long months of waiting and watching. Daily the arrival of troops, horses, mules, and baggage went on, and daily our spirits rose at the prospect of the coming advance into the enemy's country.

CHAPTER 3

Cattle Raiders

Note.—The figures in this adventure are fictional: otherwise the setting and the theme are real.

Saidi-Bin-Mohammed, native of East Africa, had been to the war a year. When the English had gone to the borders of his country to face the German enemy, Saidi had followed his white master.

One day in June, about 5 o'clock—about that time of day most pleasant in Africa, when the sun is lowering in the west and losing its intensive piercing heat—Saidi, tall, and straight and athletic, was busied outside his small grass hut, cleaning his equipment and rifle with the interest and care of one who had pride in dearly loved possessions. Across the dry, bleached, much-trampled opening of the encampment, which lay in the midst of virgin bush-land, appeared the gaunt figure of a British officer. He stooped, as with age, and his dark, tanned face bore heavy traces of exposure and hardship, in the deep-lined furrows which covered his forehead, and in the fine lines that contracted to the corners of his tired eyes. But, though worn and lean, he had still about him the bearing of resolute manhood—the bearing of one who is strong to endure and conquer, even under difficulties and a merciless tropic sun. Clive Clifford had, in the old days, been a pioneer of unbound frontiers, and a hunter of big game: today he was a famous scout; a man whose knowledge and whose word carried weight in the highest quarters of command.

He approached Saidi, who smiled broadly seeing that his master, whom he held in high regard, came to him. Clifford spoke in the soft, halting consonants of the Swahili language, and addressed his *boy* in kindly manner, as a man speaking to a trusted servant. "Saidi," he said, "get ready. We go out to-night, you and I, and stay out many days. Eat food now; and be ready to leave in an hour."

Some hours before, half-a-dozen Masai warriors had run into camp to report that enemy had stolen many of their cattle, and were driving them off across the border. Clifford heard the story. He knew the country the enemy were plundering, and volunteered at once to go in pursuit. It was an adventure dear to his heart.

At dusk they quietly left the noisy, troop-filled camp—the master leading, Saidi following. They were mounted on wiry, donkey-like Somali mules, animals so small that they appeared disproportionately overburdened with their load and their well-filled saddle-bags. But in this they were deceptive. Clifford knew them, from long experience, to have no equal in animal transport in the country. Tireless little animals they were, grit to the back-bone, and strong to endure long, heart-breaking treks.

Clifford was fully armed, with rifle and cartridge-filled bandolier; as was his boy. A *slouch* hat, a sleeveless khaki shirt, open at the neck; and a pair of shorts, leaving the scarred, sun-burned knees bare and free, was Clifford's uniform. Undress, but near to coolness and comfort as possible—and protective in colour, for, when smothered in dust, as all would soon be, his light drill khaki would be as a tussock of sun-bleached grass or a hillock of sand, if danger bid him take cover. . . .

Some hours later, after making good time in the cool of early night, the travellers began to work clear of the low thorn-bush, and emerged into open, somewhat mountainous country. Clifford was travelling west now, and travelling fast; feeling his way over the country to some distant prearranged destination. Saidi, the expert guide, was out in the lead—for no white man has eyes or hearing equal to the black in his native country. Both travellers were dismounted and led their mules. They wound their way through tall valley grass, breast high and dust-laden; over pools of mud, long sun-baked and waterless; then out, finally, on to rising ground strewn with lava rock and volcanic boulders. It was weird wilderness country, barren of habitation—virgin and waterless as on the day of Africa's dawning.

The night progressed uneventfully. Nothing suspicious was encountered. No tracks of the cattle raiders were crossed. The air was breathlessly still, and it was oppressively hot in the valleys.

Toward midnight the waning moon drooped lower and lower on the horizon—and went out. Travelling then became slower and more wary; occasionally man or mule stumbled over a boulder painfully and noisily in the breathless darkness. No conversation passed between man and servant. Tirelessly they padded on, each certain of the other's knowledge almost as animals are certain of the bypaths to their lair. For them the night held little mystery. They were startled not by the grim silhouettes of zebra, or hartebeest, when, at a dozen yards, they chanced upon game herds which galloped off into the night like riderless squadrons. Nor did the whir of wings and frightened cackle of guinea-fowl, disturbed at their very feet, more than startle the mules to one brief backward jerk of their bridle reins.

Day was dawning when Saidi, who had for some hours been following an obscure track through the dark with his lynx eyes, gave a grunt of satisfaction as a gap loomed visible between two dull grey hills in front. Soon they entered a narrow pass and prepared to make camp in the hidden cavity between the hills.

Here was water, and camp, and the first halt in the march; for a dry rocky river-bed, cut by the torrents of the brief rainy season, ran down the pass, and there, in a deep pocket in the solid rock, worn smooth and circular as a gigantic porridge pot, was a pool of water, green-slimed and stagnant, it is true, but priceless, nevertheless, in the sun-parched desert. The mules were off-saddled, rubbed down, and fed; and picketed under cover of the hill-side—for they were now in country where the raiders might be encountered, and every precaution was being taken to lie low and outwit the enemy.

Saidi busied himself over a small smokeless fire, making tea for his master, while Clifford lay idly on the ground watching the doves and grass-finches, which in thousands were endlessly arriving at the water-hole to drink, fearless of human presence in their haste and need to quench their thirst.

"Water far, Saidi," said Clifford, pointing to the fluttering flock over the pool. "Birds come long distance to drink here?"

"Yes, *Bwana*" (master), answered Saidi. "No other water nearer than one day."

By turns Clifford and Saidi slept and kept watch throughout the day. The camp was in the foothills of a low range, east of the Guaso Nyero Valley. Away to the west, out to the Nguruman Mountains, blue in the farthermost distance, lay the far-reaching Guaso Nyero Valley; and it was on this great plain, somewhere, that the enemy were raiding the Masai cattle. Clifford hardly expected to find trace of the enemy until after another march, when he would be well over the western side of the valley, and where he knew there was a sluggish stream and an abundance of water—that physical essential, to man and beast, anywhere in the land. But he was taking no risks—nothing for granted—for a little mistake meant life or death to the enterprise, if not to himself.

So all day long watchful eyes scanned the western plain, but only to be rewarded with the familiar sight of occasional dust-clouds; sometimes kicked up by the feet of moving

51

game, such as zebra, hartebeest, wildebeest, or buffalo; and sometimes the sport of a whirlpool gust of wind which swiftly sweeps the ground, finally to rear a thin spiral dust-column tapering from the ground to a point high in the sky.

Toward sundown three Masai were sighted, worming their way in and out of the long yellow grass toward the waterhole. They came from the west, and were travelling hurriedly, perhaps fearfully—for ever and anon the rear man of the trio would cast a hasty backward glance over his shoulder. Cunningly, in fear that foe might be at the water, they swung wide of the pass before approaching, and lay down while one of their number started to steal forward in the grass to investigate. But a shout from Saidi, and then an exchange of a reassuring word or two, brought them speedily to their feet, and into camp.

Like all of the Masai race, they were strange, red-skinned fellows, those wandering cattle men of the open uplands; wholly naked but for a loin cloth, and physical pictures of the aboriginal of the plain. For arms, they had each a long assegai, and a large mat-laced shield. They were covered with dust—otherwise, their bearing conveyed nothing untoward. It would be difficult to guess that beneath those features, cool and collected, expressionless, almost sullen, there lurked the emotions of men who had been near to death an hour or two ago.

After they had all drunk copiously of water, at a little distance from Clifford, they squatted on the ground with their knees drawn up under their chins, and told their hurried, broken story.

In their own language they arrived crudely and directly at essential facts.

"Germans, master, many Germans," said their spokesman, showing, for the first time, a spark of excitement. "This day, when sun there"—pointing to the mid-horizon south-east "our cattle quiet—we cooking food; at that time he come— one German, two German, three German, on horse—after him come plenty Askaris (native soldiers) driving many cattle—cattle footsore, for long way he made go too fast. One German ride among us—he got small gun, and promise shoot to kill if we try to run away—Askaris come soon and bind our hands with cord; then one man stay to watch us. In little while Germans make fire and eat—plenty talk—plenty bottle (beer)—German pleased. By and by German sleep. By and by Askaris, who watch us, he sleep too—he plenty tired. Headman, he find stone beneath him and work cord binding hands against it. Sometime, cord cut—soon, then, we all free. We crawl in grass, far—afterwards we wait and watch. When the sun there" (pointing to sun's position about three hours later) "German wake find no boy. Plenty noise Askari who watch us, he get plenty beating afterwards they tie him prisoner—German afraid we run far and fast and go tell British. Soon German go—driving all cattle—our cattle too. But other cattle tired, master, he no go quick now; and German near his own country. He go Shombole and Lake Natron, one day's trail, after that, soon he reach big German camp."

Clifford was lost in thought—the Masai had ceased talking, and the youngest of them, a mere lad, had fallen asleep, hunched up awkwardly, on the bare, hard ground, weary beyond further caring. Saidi, who had listened attentively to all, moved off and busied himself over a fire and his master's evening meal. The customary evening breeze had not arisen, it was close and oppressively hot, and a subdued spirit lay over the land. Clifford restlessly stirred the gravel beneath his feet, lost in his conjectures. He was wide awake and his keen, roving eyes betokened an intelligent mind stirred to unusual degree. The enterprise had taken on a serious aspect. Clifford had anticipated, if he were fortunate, he would run up against a small raiding party of one or two whites and a native soldier or two. His original difficulty, he thought, would be to track them, and overtake them. He found himself, instead, pitted against four whites and some dozen armed Askaris, whom he could head off, on their southward trail, in a single night's march.

The odds were great—too great—but he was too far from his base to call for reinforcements; he must go on as he was, or return to camp mortified at having had the enemy within reach while admitting his inability to strike.

Clifford rose impatiently to his feet and paced to and fro.

But slowly a new resolution crept into his face and bearing, and at last his mind was made up. He called his boy. "Saidi," he said, "I'm not going to stop here and go back; I'm going on. I may not fight, for the Germans are many; but I mean to get as near to the raiders as I can, and, for the rest, trust to luck and opportunity. You, Saidi, are free to go back if you please. I cannot order you to run the risks ahead against such odds, This is my *show*."

But Saidi was staunch and true. "Where master go, I want to go—me not afraid," he said; and indeed he did not look one whit abashed—rather was there a new-found pride in his bearing.

The undertaking thus promoted, Clifford, with mind relieved, partook of the substantial meal which Saidi had prepared. They then saddled the mules, and were ready again to take up the trail of the raiders. The exhausted Masai were given some food from Saidi's saddle-bags and told to sleep at the water-hole for the night. They were directed to follow Clifford's tracks in the morning, and remain at a discreet distance from the enemy, unless sent for.

On leaving camp Clifford headed out into the south-west, for it was his intention to cut across the German line of flight, well in front of them, and, before daybreak, to hide among the low *kopjes* east of Lake Natron. To carry this out he must travel hard all night. Accordingly the pace he set off at was determined and sustained. Man and beast perspired freely as they toiled onward; for relentlessly the night breeze held off, and the still, humid air hung, like the vapours of a hot-house, over the breathless valley. To add to the discomfort, the trotting mules raised, from the dust-laden grass, a fine dust which remained suspended in the air to irritate the nostrils and throats of the travellers, and induce a quenchless, vexing thirst. However, until midnight Clifford held on his course unfalteringly. At that hour, just before the moon went down, he halted to rest and ease the saddle-girths of the tired mules.

Half an hour later he resumed the journey; but on foot, now that it was pitch dark, the mules led, and faithful, tireless Saidi out in front trailing, with his keen eyes, over unseen landmarks, for the low hills his master had named.

They were in rough country now—rough with awkward boulders and ragged lava rocks. Moreover, the travellers were repeatedly confronted with yawning chasms—deep, dry, tortuous river-beds—which barred their path. In the inky darkness to surmount these obstacles was difficult and delaying, and Clifford cursed them roundly while he *barked* his shins in scrambling up and down banks of unknown depth, forcing his way across in the wake of Saidi, whose presence he could feel rather than see.

To add to their difficulties, the mules were restless. They were in fear of lions, for twice, away northward, the night stillness had vibrated with the awesome *whouh—whouh— whouh—whouh——whouh—whouh—wwho—wwho—wwho— wwho—wwho—wwho* of the King of Beasts. The sound brought terror to the hearts of the mules, and delayed progress. But, at the same time, it brought a note of good cheer to the party, for to the experienced ears of Clifford and Saidi the lions' roar was a good omen, coming, as it did, from the north-west of their position: for they guessed that the lions were among the beasts of prey following in the track of the trekking cattle, ready to drag down and devour the weaker ones which became too exhausted to go on and were outcast from the herd. If the surmise was correct, Clifford felt sure he was cutting in well ahead of the cattle raiders—and only that result could compensate him for the toil of travelling this ghastly country in the dark.

About 4 a.m. Clifford, in spite of short halts, was feeling

done up with his exertions in keeping pace with Saidi. Hardened though he was, he inwardly admitted he was about finished on this trek. He halted and whistled peculiarly to Saidi, who stopped likewise. Saidi came back to his master, apparently cool and tireless as ever, and sure of his un-traced road. Clifford asked him how far he thought they were from the hills. In answer, Saidi pointed into the darkness a little to the left. "There, master," he said, "close now—river we cross last, near to hills—soon we camp."

Thus cheered, they started on the final tramp; but Saidi's hills were deceptive, his *short distance* stretched out to a good two miles before the tired party reached their chosen hiding-place.

At the first inkling of dawn, Clifford moved well into the hills and secreted the mules in the bottom of a valley thickly grown with cactus. From there Clifford and Saidi made their way to a spur overlooking the plain on the west and north. Here they concealed themselves among some acacia bushes, after they had made sure that, in the event of discovery, there was a line of retreat down either slope of the spur to thicker cover—whence their hidden rifles could put up a reasonable defence against odds, if need be.

From where he stood in the early morning dawn, Clifford had a wonderful view of the wild life and of the country. Below him a small herd of graceful antelope, known as Grant's gazelle, was browsing quietly in the immediate foreground of the plain—a plain of dry, buff-coloured grass which stretched some two miles to the west, to the shores of Lake Natron. In the intermediate distance was a great herd of unsymmetrical hartebeest (buck of size and colour of red deer), and pony-like zebra, moving along, in ever-changing attitudes, busy on their morning feed, and lending life and colour to the peaceful scene. Along the shores of Lake Natron, white soda deposit glistened like silver in the lightening day, whilst the waters of the lake appeared dyed in pink where countless flamingoes rested. A mile or two up the valley, at the head of Lake Natron, and to the east of the swamp of tall green grass which is there, rugged old Shombole mountain stood prominent with its furrowed surface of deep ravines and back-bone ridges, the whole overawed by the sheer cliff face, and the inaccessible plateau at the towering crest, of the most westerly range. In many places the outer slopes of Shombole were buff with the dry, yellow grass of the plains, but in the ravines, and on sheltered slopes, dark-green foliage grew where overcrowded masses of impenetrable cactus had found root, and an existence, amongst the rocks.

Meantime there was no sign of the enemy—nothing moved, except droves of game in this hunter's paradise.

Clifford estimated that he was an hour or two ahead of the raiders, and soon he dozed in the cool of the morning—leaving Saidi on guard. He trusted the boy completely, for the experience of long months had proved him always faithful and fearless to serve. Faithful as a wonderful dog was Saidi, and "greater faith hath no man." Saidi worshipped his master.

Some hours passed—Clifford had fallen into profound sleep after his long night's exertion, for he was more easily tired now than in the old days before he knew the impairing ravages of fever. The heightened day found Saidi still at his post. But he was now tense and alert, and his eyes were eagerly fixed on a cloud of dust approaching from the north. There were the raiders! Of that he was sure; for he had seen a horseman break off to the right, clear of the dust, for a moment or two. However, he would not wake his master yet; the raiders were far out at present, and the cattle they herded moved very slowly.

In a short time, however, he espied two horsemen riding forward, at an easy gallop, clear of the herd. They were probably coming on ahead to select their noon camp, confident that the plain was uninhabited but by themselves. Seeing this, Saidi woke Clifford, who was instantly on his feet, and eager to sight the enemy.

Immediately a daring scheme of attack flashed through Clifford's mind—the enemy were playing into his hands in separating their forces. Hastily he lifted his rifle, spoke a few excited words to Saidi, and started to steal through the grass down to the plain on the west. Once on the plain they scrambled and crawled, under cover of a dry, shallow rivulet, seeking to reach the probable line over which the advancing horsemen would pass. Over a mile they laboured, slowly, awkwardly, until, scratched, torn, and breathless with their mad haste, they lay still; near to the place on which the enemy were bearing.

As fate would have it, the horsemen bore straight down on them, utterly unaware of danger. Clifford whispered to Saidi that he was to shoot the nearest horse at the same time as he (Clifford) fired. With their rifles in the grass, and with heads low, they watched and waited. Grim was the expression on their faces now, all outward excitement had gone : nerves were set, and *steeled* against the coming effort. Suddenly—when the horses were barely fifteen yards away, Clifford whispered tersely, "Now!" Simultaneously, both rifles spoke, and all was violent struggle and confusion on the ground in front. Clifford stood upright and fired quickly again. Then, harshly, he called out a command in German, while like a flash his rifle swung to his right and remained aimed at its object. Unmoved, he ordered Saidi from his hiding-place. Both horses were down, and the nearest German; the other German had his hands up, covered by Clifford. Saidi removed the German's rifle, which lay on the ground where it had been thrown when the horse, with its rider, fell. The prisoner was then speedily bound and gagged, so that he could not warn the others, and concealed in the rivulet ditch. The other German was dead, and both horses. The horses could not be moved, so, to disguise them from sight at a distance, the carcases were hastily covered with prairie grass.

Meantime the main body of the enemy was approaching,

but, luckily, at a slow pace. The scene enacted had been lost to the other raiders, for a low rise lay between them and the ground, gently falling to the lake, where Clifford had ambushed the leaders. The rifle shots they must have heard, but, as they were not expecting enemy, they would probably think that their comrades were after game, for meat for their natives, as was common practice.

After making certain that the prisoner was securely bound and concealed, and unable to move away, Clifford now moved hastily forward; his intention being to reach the protection of a small knoll about six hundred yards nearer to the approaching enemy and away from the condemning signs of catastrophe. But before he got there, dust, over the rise, warned him and his boy to take cover. So they lay on the open veldt, in the hay grass, not daring to move to better cover, for, at any instant now, horsemen, or keen-sighted Askari, might appear in view. Lying there, Clifford gave his orders to Saidi, who grinned still over the success of their first attack. "Fire like H———, Saidi! at Askaris—make plenty noise—make him think plenty British here. Make him run!"

Clifford was confident of the outcome now, and eager for the fray. By an extraordinary piece of luck the white opposition had been evened up and now he had the advantage of surprise, and the consequent target for his deadly rifle.

Slowly the raiders appeared in view over the rising ground, and drew on. Together the Germans scanned the plain ahead, but beyond a word or two they, apparently, did not trouble about the non-appearance of their comrades—they thought, no doubt, that theirs was only a momentary disappearance behind some low ridge in the distance.

The raiders sat their horses idly, and watched the tired cattle being herded on; they swore at their Askaris and urged them, time without number, to lash on the many laggards. Apparently they were weary of their work, and tired of the trek.

Clifford and Saidi were waiting breathlessly. The herd was a bit to the right, but was going to pass them at about fifty yards. Steadily they drew on. Again the rifles were ready in the grass; again Clifford's terse, "now!" was whispered, and startling shots rang out. And then the scene was like a battle. Shots poured from their hidden haven in the grass, as fast as they could load and fire, simply to disguise their strength and frighten the blacks.

Clifford had brought down his first man, but the second white he missed, as his startled horse plunged and threw the rider. For a time the German replied vigorously to their fire, but luckily he couldn't see through the grass, and no bullet got home. Suddenly he rose and scrambled on to one of the horses and galloped off. Twice Clifford fired and missed, but at the third shot the German crumpled up and slid limply from his mount. Clifford now ran forward, and caught the remaining horse; Saidi following at his heels. Shots whistled and cracked around them, but all were wide of the mark; for the Askari is a poor marksman. Into the blacks rode Clifford, reckless and wild, driving them to panic and confusion. Two went down with his first shots, the rest, five in number, leapt from the grass and fled in frantic disorder. One more fell, sprawling, to Clifford's marksmanship, and another was winged. But by that time the remainder had spread and got farther afield, and Clifford gave up the chase, afraid to get too far away from Saidi, who might be in difficulties.

Returning, Clifford found Saidi broadly smiling, as was his wont when greatly pleased. He had accounted for three Askaris. Clifford praised the boy—though he seldom gave praise to a native—and told him, now, to make "plenty big feed" for himself, and then to sleep—the boy had had no rest since the day before.

While Saidi busied himself lighting a fire, Clifford counted the cost.

One German was dead, one wounded. Four Askaris were

dead, and three wounded. After he had gone back and brought the prisoner to camp, Clifford attended to the wounded. When that gruesome work was finished, he sought a vantage-point on a rise, and, from there, sent three piercing whistles out over the plain.

He was soon rewarded by the sight of natives, showing in the grass, about a mile to the east. They were the three Masai left behind overnight; and he signalled to them to come on.

In a short time the Masai came up.

Fear was first in their approach, then astonishment, when they sighted the destruction of the enemy, and Clifford and Saidi in complete possession of the cattle. Their usually passive faces broke into broad smiles, they gesticulated excitedly in their exclamations over the extraordinary scene; and, finally, they came, one by one, before Clifford, to voice their timid gratitude, and to salaam profoundly, as vassals to their lord. He was, in their eyes, indeed a mighty and wonderful white chief.

A *chit* was written to G.H.Q. asking for a mounted patrol to be sent out to conduct the cattle back to a safe area, and a Masai runner was dispatched with it to camp—with instructions, also, to send word to his tribe to furnish some men to dig graves.

The remaining Masai counted the cattle. They numbered close on seven hundred head—a substantial meat ration for the Europeans over the border, if the raid had succeeded. Clifford directed the Masai to drive the cattle slowly back to the Guaso Nyero River, and to wait for him at the bend beyond the northern slopes of Mount Shombole. Before leaving, they released the hidden mules, and drove them also to water.

* * * * * * * *

Three days later an officer and a native soldier rode into the British camp, dust-covered and with clothes torn. Dismounting, the officer left his mule in the care of the native and passed on to the encampment of G.H.Q.

Down the dry dust-thick lanes of the camp stalked the well-known figure of the famous scout—the lean, the brown, the worn bush-man, scarred and tired with exposure and climate—a thing of the wild world and the silent places—unassuming, almost shy. But, on a thousand lips the news flew among the troops that Clive Clifford was back—and glad men came from their tents to cheer him past.

And Saidi, unsaddling the mules in the horse lines, hearing the welcome, smiled in content.

CHAPTER 4

The First Advance

The dusty road through dense tropical thorn-bush followed the *lie* of the mountain, and to approach Longido West you came round the bend from the west, and swung easterly, to find the camp, an irregular, partly cleared space in the midst of trees. The camp, with cunning purpose, was under cover, for it was within the timber line, which hung densely in colour and form along, and all around, the mountain base. Beyond, at no great distance to the south and west, the bush terminated, and open yellow veldt stretched far out to the hill-marked distance where sheltered the considerable town of Aruscha.

The whole was a wilderness country, neither bush nor veldt held human creature! All that lived was of nature's giving! In the forest of thorns, and by the mountain-fed streamlet which gave the camp sparingly of priceless water, bird, insect, and plant life, in myriad forms, were habited in abundance. Beyond the jungle of low-stature trees, the veldt lay in expressionless vagueness and silence, with but the slow, dark movement of a small number of ostrich and wildebeest, and the flight of a ranging vulture, to attract and hold the wandering eye.

And it was here that our forces were congregating, over the German border, under the south-western continuance of Longido Mountain. We had been days in coming, and we had come from many places—British, South African, Indian, and native African—and we knew by the unwanted stir of traffic that there was *something on*. A day passed, two days, and still the gathering grew! Troops and transport—ox wagons, mule wagons, and motors—and the hundred-and-one oddments that accompany a large force, came into view at the clearing entrance, passed down the road and camped, and thenceforth became part of us. In time, it came to be the evening of the second day, and a great stir arose in camp.

Orders were out: we were to commence the advance to-morrow! Suppressed excitement was in the air! Down the dust-smothered road, as I passed to camp, there trooped to water a hurrying continual line of thirsty, road-tired, sad-vis-aged horses, mules, and oxen, accompanied by gesticulating, chattering, khaki-clad attendants. The men were discussing the news, and the prospect ahead, in many different ways and in different tongues of English, Dutch, Hindu, and Swahili. It was nigh to the common hour of peacefulness—that is, *peace* as near as it is ever realised in the army—when half-clad, begrimed, talkative soldiers grub and wash up around the evening camp fires. But tonight there was no peace. Ser-geants were calling out orders on every rustle of the wind, fa-tigue parties were falling-in here, there, and everywhere. Final preparations were in full swing, and—what use to deny it?—fuss and confusion held sway, as if in devilish glee. Rations, the most vital care of the army, were discussed and arranged. Kits to go, 25 lb. per man, including his blanket and spare boots, and surplus kits to be left behind were packed and loaded on wagons, or stored. Sick men, and men not particularly robust, were sorted out and detailed for garrison, for commanders realise that only the very fittest can endure the hardship of a long trek in Africa. Finally all was arranged and the sleep of night settled on the camp.

Next day we were off to the south on a narrow dust-laden track. We were an infantry column, a column made up of variously dressed soldiers of different races, a column of various kind and equipment, eloquent of the brotherhood of colonies. We streamed out in column of route, after scouts had preceded us by half an hour or so. The 129th Baluchis, olive-hued Indian soldiers in turbans and loose-kneed trousers, were in advance; then their maxim battery of gunners and side-burdened, bridle-led mules. Then came the 29th Punjabis, another regiment of similar kind, followed closely by some battalions of South African artillery—a bold array of gun-carriages and ammunition wagons, each drawn by eight span of sturdy South-American-bred mules, and driven by reckless Cape boys mounted on the line of near mules. Then followed more infantry, the 25th Royal Fusiliers, of familiar face and colour, of our own kind, but soiled and sunburnt with long exposure; the 1st King's African Rifles, well-trained natives of stalwart appearance, khaki-clad as the rest, but with distinctive dark-blue puttees and light close-fitting headgear. And so on, and so on, down the line, except that one might mention the ammunition column in the rear, a long line of two-wheeled carts, drawn by two span of patient, slow-gaited oxen. In the rear, trailing far behind, came the miscellaneous transport—some motors, large four-wheeled mule-wagons, Scotch carts, and water carts, an assortment of varied, somewhat gipsy-like kind. The wagons, which were most in evidence, and which carry from three thousand to four thousand pounds, were drawn by ten span of mules, or by sixteen to twenty span of oxen, and all were ordered and driven by capable management of men from South Africa, who had long experience in trekking in their own country. In all it was probably a column of a fighting strength of from 4,000 to 5,000 men, with its necessary large following of accoutrements.

When the column reached far out into the grass-grown, sandy plain—for it was open highland here—one could look back, almost as far as the eye could distinguish, and see the course of the column, as the fine line of a sinuous thread drawn across the blank space of an incomplete map! Today, the map was marked; tomorrow, the thin dust-line would be gone onward, and the desert veldt would again lie reposed in vagueness.

Thus did we leave our harbour of safety to venture far into the enemy's country on *the long trek*; to travel amidst dust, and dryness, and heat, for many days.

It was on a Sunday morning, the 5th of March, 1916, that the advance began. This column leaving Longido was to operate round the west of Kilimanjaro and finally converge on Moschi, the terminal of the Usambara railway—the only railway in the northern area of German territory. The column was acting in conjunction with large forces operating, also on the border, away to the east of Kilimanjaro: forces which were largely South African, and that were opposite the long-standing enemy line defending Taveta and barring the main thoroughfare into German territory. This marked the commencement of the offensive campaign under General Smuts—an offensive that time proved was to last twenty-one months before German East Africa was to be cleared of the enemy and completely in our hands.

However, as I have said, one Sunday morning, at the beginning of March, found us moving out on the big game, eagerly, and with a great gladness to be *up and doing*.

The column travelled east along the line of Longido Hill, then struck south across the fiat, sandy plain before us until the shelter of the Sheep Hills was reached. Here the column was halted under the northern slopes of the hills, thus making use of the protection which they afforded from observation from the south—for the south held ever the danger of the enemy. The column had trekked about eight miles across trackless country, making a road as they went merely by the commotion and pressure of wheels and of thousands of feet of troops and their transport animals. Marching was unpleasant in the soft, powdered dust which lay ankle-deep underfoot, and was kicked in the air in a hanging cloud to choke both throat and nostrils, and adhere to every visible part of one's clothing.

Under the Sheep Hills we lay in the heat of the sun, waiting our orders. At 6.30 p.m. the column moved out on a long night march. A two hours' halt was called at midnight, but otherwise we trekked steadily on all through the night. At midnight, detachments went off on our left flank to attack at dawn the enemy post on Nagasseni Hill. The enemy were engaged, but the fight was short-lived, and in due course the hill was occupied by our troops. The main column encountered no opposition, though opposition had been expected at the Engare Naniuki water.

The column camped at 10.30 the following morning at water at Engare Naniuki. We had travelled all night into the south over a level sandy plain, covering, roughly, twenty miles. Entrenchments were dug in camp, and the swamp grass, bordering the water-holes, was burnt. Camp was unmasked to all eyes, friend or foe, by a continually rising cloud of fine chalk-like lava sand. Profusion of troops and transport were everywhere, and made an animated picture while moving here and there on quest of their unending duties.

I picked up two young hares (*sungura*) in camp, paralysed with fear at finding themselves surrounded by such overwhelming commotion. Overhead, many flocks of sand-grouse passed in the morning and evening; apparently they haunt these plains in their migrations.

The following morning we moved out at 8 o'clock and made slow progress during the march. The column skirted the river-course of Engare Naniuki and passed through open country. A long delay was caused getting the column across the *drift* at Nagasseni Bridge, when we intercepted the Aruscha— Engare Nairobi road; the river was, here, about 25 feet wide and the water swift flowing. The bridge over the river had been destroyed before our arrival. The column, in the late afternoon, camped, when across the Engare Naniuki, at Nagasseni.

Nagasseni, which had been hastily evacuated, was a prominent hill with a small *boma* and fort on the crest commanding the river and the bridge. At 2.30 in the morning the camp was stirred afoot, and the column moved out in the dark an hour later. The travelling was east, then south-east, through fairly level country commanded by many cone-shaped bare *kopjes*. We are still free of bush country. Today we march through forsaken desert, sparsely grass-grown, and of a surface nature of metallic lava crusts. A small party of enemy was engaged, on our left front, about noon. The enemy fired on our mounted advance scouts from a low *kopje* which they occupied. But our scouts had previously sighted the enemy, and had sent back word to the column. Mountain battery guns, already trained on the target, opened fire the instant the enemy showed his hand, and with deadly shooting put the enemy to flight in no time, followed by rounds of vicious shrapnel. It proved to be a mere outpost of enemy reported at thirty-five strong.

All are beginning to wonder where we are to *bump* the enemy. Is there to be no resistance offered to an advance from this side of Kilimanjaro? Has an advance here been thought impossible? Is it completely a surprise?

Soon after the short moment of excitement, above mentioned, Geraragua River was reached, and camp was pitched on the north bank. Here our position was entrenched, and camp for the night prepared.

Next day we spent in camp while a convoy returned to Engare Nairobi to assist in bringing forward rations, which were being delayed owing to the heavy half-broken tracks. Near here, at Kakowasch, an enemy camp, hastily evacuated, was found among the bush of the Kilimanjaro foothills. This was set fire to and burned so that the grass huts could not be reoccupied.

The following day the column moved out at noon—our destination said to be Ngombe, which is across the Aruscha line of the enemy's retreat from Moschi, should the eastern forces attack it from the Taveta side. We travelled until dark through level country, pimpled with numerous pygmy hills; breaking road through the country as we went. About darkening we entered bush country, which offered splendid concealment to the enemy, but they did not put in an appearance. About this time, however, some of our artillery, who were having difficulty in getting along on the heavy tracks, were attacked by the enemy in the open, some distance in our rear. Forward, with the column, the rifle-fire was heard, and the boom of our thirteen-pounders. Detachments were ordered to retire and reinforce the rear. Our battalion went back about three miles, but did not go into action, as the enemy by that time had been beaten off. Again we moved on in the darkness, and about 3 a.m. rejoined the column. It had been uncertain, awkward marching, the night was very dark, the track broken, and heavy with dust. About the time we rejoined the column it began to rain. A halt was called, and we slept in our tracks, for the remaining three hours, until daylight—then up and away again. It was bitterly cold sleeping in the open in the rain, but we were too dog-tired to care. A number of horses and mules are now dying by the roadside with horse sickness and tsetse fly. Mosquitoes numerous since entering the bush. Marched about eighteen miles today.

Saturday, 11th March—Just one week since we left Longido. Marched at 2 p.m., heading south through the bush, with Kilimanjaro Mountain on our left, and Meru Mountain on our right. Towards dusk, on reaching open country, the column swung easterly and crossed the plain, pursuing a line parallel with the southern slopes of Kilimanjaro, but well away from the mountain. The German town of Moschi was sighted away to the north-east, and eager were the eyes that witnessed it, because there was probably our objective and the enemy. About dusk, scouts engaged in a short bout of firing with opposing scouts, but soon the bush was *all clear*. Marched until

9 p.m. and camped, before Kilimanjaro, on River Sanja. Fires were observed between us and Moschi, and were thought to be those of the East African Mounted Rifles, who were reconnoitring nearer in to the mountain base. Marched about fifteen miles today.

"Stand to" was at 5 o'clock on Sunday morning, but dawn broke undisturbed. A few shots were fired by our sentries overnight at prowling scouts. Part of column moved out at 9 a.m.; and returned in evening, without having been in action. Our present camp is on the Aruscha road, about five miles from Ngombe. The column is now about sixty miles away from its starting-point at Longido.

Marched on Monday for Masai Kraal, hoping there to intercept the enemy's retreat from Moschi. Reached Ngombe about 11 a.m. A number of houses were still inhabited, by Goanese and Greeks, and they had white flags erected to protect themselves from attack. The small river Kware flowed through the village. Transport and considerable artillery were left behind here, while the column continued eastward on the low road or, more properly, track, to Moschi. The bush is now becoming more luxuriantly tropical in country that is apparently well watered. Marched until 2 a.m. in the dark, through rain, and over a track narrow and unused. On camping everyone was so done up that fires were allowed for warmth, and to make tea. Few of us could sleep, we were so very wet, and the remainder of the night was spent cowering over our fires in poor endeavour to keep some circulation alive in our numbed bodies. Marched about fifteen miles today.

The following day, in the early morning, our course was changed, and the column marched direct for Moschi, news having been received that the town had been evacuated and was occupied by South African forces from the eastern column. During the. march our column forded four rivers in the course of the day—the Kikafu, the Weruweru, the Kiladera, and the Garanga. It is slow, patience-trying work transporting animals and wagons through such river-drifts; not one or two heavily burdened mules, not one or two wagons, had to be coaxed down steep banks, and across the ford, and up the opposite bank, but the endless number of an entire column. However, in the end the last river was passed, and we marched into Moschi just after dark, a weary and footsore column; both man and beast thoroughly done up. Torrential rain fell all night, and all were very thankful for the shelter of the various buildings and barns into which we were crowded. But even then our sleep was a broken one, lying on the cold hard floor, or on the ground, without blanket covering. For the past three days we have been without our kits or blankets, only our bare rations having been transported with us in our haste onwards.

Moschi—which is the Swahili for smoke, and which aptly refers to the mists daily hanging over Kilimanjaro Mountain top—had been captured without any resistance, though it had been thought that the enemy would make a long stand there. It proved an extensive, well-built town, nestling in the pleasant and picturesque surroundings of the Kilimanjaro foothills. A mile or so above the new town were the old fort and residences of Old Moschi. Coffee and rubber were extensively grown in the district, and well-developed plantations abounded in the neighbourhood of the town. There was a large civil population left in the town at the time of occupation, principally natives, Goanese, and Greeks.

On the 15th, 16th, and 17th March we lay in Moschi resting, while it daily, and gaily, rained in torrents. Apparently the rainy season had begun in this locality.

On the evening of the 18th, however, all was again stir and movement, and the column marched out at dusk on the good *made* road that strikes south-east to Muë Hill. We marched pleasantly all night, for it was dry overhead and the moon was full. We reached Muë Hill at 4 a.m. and slept on the roadside for a brief three hours; clad only in our shirts, as we had marched out. After our brief spell of rest the wagons and pack-mules were loaded up, and we stood ready to march at a moment's notice. While waiting, some dead horses were burnt by the roadside, for the poor animals continue to die in considerable numbers each day, and if not burnt soon create, in the heat of the sun, a vile penetrating smell, repulsive to all who pass. The column marched out at 1 p.m. in a southerly direction on the road to Kahe, which was a railway station some distance down the Moschi-Tanga line. Our advance guard engaged the enemy in the thick bush, which bordered either side of the road, at about 3 p.m. and firing kept up steadily for about half an hour. From there on we intermittently engaged the enemy, who were retiring in good order and taking up fresh positions about every half-mile.

About 2 p.m. aeroplanes from the eastern forces were sighted coming out from Taveta, and they flew over our front. They were trying to locate the enemy's position ahead, and the direction of their retirement. All the afternoon heavy big-gun firing was heard, seemingly from somewhere west of Kitowo Mountains. The eastern column is evidently in action today, while we, too, are at last in touch with the main enemy forces.

Camped for the night at Store—an open space with a few long-limbed cocoa-nut palms therein, and enclosed on all sides by thick forest, with the Defu River immediately on our right. No blankets to-night, and no fires possible on account of the proximity of the enemy. Camp fired on on three occasions overnight, but disturbances were short-lived. These alarms were at 2 a.m., 4 a.m., and at daylight.

The following day we remained in camp. No rations until noon, for owing to bad river-drifts, and wagon accidents in the darkness, the toiling transport had been outpaced, and left far behind, on the past two days of trekking. Much rejoicing among the breakfastless men when rations turned up. Aeroplanes scouting south of us in forenoon. The enemy, under the command of Kraut, is said to be holding the entire front on the Ruwu River, between Kahe Station (extreme west of line) and the marshes west of Mokinni Mountain (extreme east of line).

About 5 p.m. an enemy patrol crept up to the river where our troops were bathing and watering their animals, and opened fire on them. Confusion ensued on the river-bank. Unarmed bathers beat a precipitous retreat; mules and horses broke away in all directions. One of our men, stark naked, rushing back to our trench line for his arms, was amusingly confronted by the General and the Colonel of our battalion, who stopped him to inquire the cause of the disturbance. The poor fellow felt much abashed, and, no doubt, wished the ground would open up and swallow him. The firing soon ceased, and the excitement it had caused gradually quietened down. But peace was doomed to be short-lived, for at 8 a.m. at a suddenly given signal, tremendous fire swept the camp and startled everyone to frightful wakefulness. Bugle calls of the enemy rang out immediately after the first burst of firing, and thenceforward a deafening, close-grappling, vicious battle held forth. Time after time the enemy came on at our trench line, always to be held up and driven back. In all they made about twenty charges in frontal attack, and were once almost into our line. The engagement raged without pause for about four hours. The frontal attack, which could be rapidly rein-forced from the road from the south, was the heaviest, but both flanks, at the same time, underwent considerable pres-sure, though from a farther range. German bugles sounded the advance from time to time, whenever there was a lull in the firing, as if the moment's pause had been to take in breath for a fresh effort; and when one bugle sounded, the call would be caught up and repeated all around us in the darkness of the bush. The enemy fire, fortunately for us, was bad, for it was mostly too high, also many bullets were obstructed in their flight through the dense forest. Otherwise, our casualties must have been extremely heavy, for many of the column were without any trench cover, and lay exposed on the open ground. As it was our casualty return, eventually, was only three killed and seventeen wounded, and a number of horses destroyed, while, next day, the enemy were reported to have had fully one hundred casualties.

Next day—the memorable 21st of March, 1916—in the early morning, our column was reinforced from the eastern command with two battalions of South African Infantry, armoured cars, and some field guns. Orders had been received to attack Kahe. Our right was to be on the main road, when we advanced into battle. It transpired that General Van Deventer's mounted brigade had passed through Moschi last night, and was to advance on the right flank and attack west and south of Kahe Station, while, at the same time, the eastern column was to operate along the line of the Himo River on the left flank.

Our column moved out at 9 a.m. Contact with the enemy was very soon found thereafter. At 11 a.m. our artillery opened fire on the enemy positions, while meantime our fighting line had formed and advanced slowly until about 400 to 800 yards off the enemy's entrenched and prepared positions in the bottle-neck formed by the Soko-Nassai River at its junction with the Defu River. Here our forces were held, and the battle raged bitterly for some hours. Some of the enemy machine-guns were faultlessly handled, and inflicted heavy casualties. The fight was across a dead-level open grass space, terminating in bush at either fighting line. It was in the bush, on the enemy's side, that their death-dealing machine-guns were concealed, and throughout the day our artillery failed to search them out. I saw those machine-gun emplacements later—there were two outstanding ones —and one proved to be on a raised platform, eight feet above ground, and skilfully concealed amongst the trees; the other was in a dug-out pit, with a fire-directing observation post in a tall tree standing just behind it. Where each gun had stood lay a huge stack of empty cartridge-cases, telling clearly that their gunners had found a big target. But where the raised gun had been, blood in all directions, and torn garments, and dead natives, told that not without payment had they held their post. But I digress. The battle raged unceasingly until dusk, with all its grime, and thirst, and heart-aching bloodshed. With darkness the firing ceased, as if by mutual consent, and immediately we commenced to strengthen our hastily dug trenches—dug during the action with bayonets, knives, hands—anything. And there they laboured, those grim, dirt- and blood-bespattered men of the firing line, while movement became general on all occupations. Ambulances and doctors were being sought on all sides, while many men passed along looking for water, in desperate need of quenching their thirst. In that bush forest, after dark, wandering parties, unfamiliar with the encampment as it lay after battle, seemed to be looking for every regiment, and water-cart, and doctor in creation. Late into the night the labours of readjustment and of organisation went on, while in the trenches dog-tired men, one by one, dropped off to sleep. About midnight peace settled over the camp, and the remainder of the night passed without further disturbance. At dawn, patrols went out and found the enemy had evacuated the entire front of prepared entrenchments, and had retired rapidly south under cover of the bush and the darkness. At the same time, news came in that General Van Deventer's mounted troops had occupied Kahe Station, and the two commanding *kopjes* to the south. So, for the time being, the storm of arms was over, and the enemy had staved off defeat by evading a prolonged battle.

At 9 a.m. our battalion moved forward and took up a new defensive line, facing the south, across the Ruwu River. South of the Ruwu River, on the left flank of the enemy's position, lay the ruins of a 4·1 naval gun, laboriously transported inland from the *Koenigsberg* battleship, which, in the early days of the war, our naval forces had crippled and rendered unseaworthy after chasing it to its lair in the mouth of the Rufiji River. About 7 o'clock on the previous night all had heard a terrific explosion, and there now lay the wreckage of it. The gun had been set up completely and with ingenious labour. Iron girders carried the heavy plank platform which received the deck mountings of the gun. Tools, and ironmongery, and rope, of ship-board nature, lay about the gun in profusion. In all construction the equipment and labour were thorough and workmanlike. The labour of carrying the material from Kahe Station, and the labour of erection, must have been colossal, one would think almost impossible. The observation post for the gun—a crow's-nest platform with a rude ladder access—was in a high thorn tree towering above all its neighbours; and during the late battle, from this look-out, they had been able to direct the fire of the gun on to both Van Deventer's column and our own. Close to the gun were the many grass huts of an encampment of some weeks' standing, while all about those dwellings were native stores of mealie-meal, peas and beans, and calabashes and empty bottles, the leavings of a settled camp suddenly unsettled.

The bridges over the Soko-Nassai and the Ruwu Rivers had been partially destroyed, and a party of us was selected to repair them, as soon as camp was established. Much of the old bridge timber was reclaimed from the floating ruins, wherever it was found to have jammed down-stream, and this saved us much labour, for otherwise make-shift timber would have had to be cut from the surrounding trees. Toward the end of the day the reconstruction was successfully completed. A rail was then run along either side of those bridges, and laced with broad banana leaves, so that transport animals would not see the drop to the river surface underneath. Grass and earth were then laid over the planking of the bridge, and again this was to assist the timid mules and cattle to face the crossing of an obstacle that they all instinctively feared.

On 23rd and 24th March, the column remained camped at Ruwu River. The day after the battle some interesting information was obtained from prisoners and is here noted: Two companies of the enemy were at Engare Nairobi at the time of our march from the border, and were to have held up our advance on Moschi. They retired on Moschi without offering any prolonged or determined resistance, and it transpired that the Major in command was severely reprimanded by the O.C. there; and took it so much to heart that he committed suicide the same night.

Sixteen companies—varying from 150 to 260 rifles per company—retired on Kahe from Moschi district.

The night attack on Store on the 20th inst. was made by three companies, while seven were held in reserve at Kahe. The enemy are stated to have had information that our strength was four infantry battalions. If that is correct, they were exceedingly courageous, or very foolish, to attack a force more than double their averred strength.

In the action before Kahe the enemy were said to have employed eight companies. After the engagement they were reported to have retired from the Ruwu front on to Lembeni, which is some twenty miles farther south on the railway. It is estimated that twenty companies have congregated at Lembeni, and that another stand is likely to be made there.

A doctor in the R.A.M.C. told me our casualties in the Kahe action were about 200. German intelligence notes, captured later, showed that their casualties had been eighteen Europeans and 146 Askaris. So that, if one recalls that we were attacking the enemy in their prepared positions, without cover for our troops, the result was not discouraging. Moreover, as I have said, their machine-guns were most skilfully handled and accounted for a large percentage of our casualties.

During the two days in camp at Ruwu, block-houses were built at the bridge crossings for the rains had seriously commenced, and the line was here to be held until it was feasible to continue the advance. During the rains it would be impossible to go on, for the country would then be impassable for transport and guns; indeed much of it would be under water. Moreover, it was necessary to lay the railway line on from our base at Maktau to link up with the railway terminus at Moschi. So, meantime, a battalion of Baluchis were detailed to hold the line on the Ruwu, while the column retired to Moschi, which had the advantage of being on higher and dryer ground, and was nearer to the base of supplies. On 25th March the column commenced the return march, through heavy rain, and on terrible roads. The rain had coagulated the loose dust into a sticky holding mud that adhered, like a weight of lead, to the marching feet. Late at night, after a very trying march, the column reached Muë Hill and camped below the hill in an open space which resembled a marsh, for it was six inches deep in mud and water. In this way we lay down and slept as best we could, and passed a bad night.

Next day, which was Sunday, we marched at dawn; again through mud and rain. Many of our battalion fell out today, unable to go on, and were picked up by the following ambulances. No evening meal last night, and no breakfast this morning; and the men are feeling the acute strain that has been put on their endurance. We reached Moschi about noon, and the battalion was billeted in deserted buildings in the town.

And there our travels for a time ended, for it transpired that we were fated to lie in Moschi for a month and a half while it rained incessantly. The first trek was over, a trek that, since crossing the frontier, had entailed, for our column, a march of some 148 miles.

CHAPTER 5

The Second Trek

On 14th May, 1916, I received orders to take the entire transport from Kibosho, west of Moschi, back to Mbuyuni, on the Taveta side, where the column was rapidly outfitting for another advance. The rains were over. Our rest at Moschi was at an end.

After a few days' hurried preparation we marched out from Mbuyuni in the afternoon of the 18th of May, and continued on the way all through the night. It was a memorable march. I happened to be temporarily in charge of battalion transport, and had to set out with a batch of *green* mules which had been allotted to me on the previous day, and some of which had never had a saddle on. All through the trek it was incessantly a case of chasing escaped mules across country, repairing broken harness, and re-saddling the rearing, frightened, stubborn brutes. I, and my comrades, spent the whole night on horseback, rounding up runaways, on the outskirts of the column, and we had our hands full. During our labours, four mules were completely lost in the dark; they had been either overrun and left far behind, or they had been caught by others. However, we got into camp in the end with two over our complement, for others had experienced the same difficulties as ourselves all along the column; and when in a tight corner, there is a popular old army maxim which says that "the Lord helps those that help themselves." So we had helped ourselves, when we found stray animals without an owner. This first day out was the worst, in dealing with the transport animals, and very soon hard work and experience had won them all over to steady-going patient beasts of burden.

The column marched in stages from Mbuyuni to Taveta, from Taveta to Himo River, and from Himo River to Kahe; the battle-field of the 21st of March, and the line at which operations ceased when the rains overtook us. From Mbuyuni to Kahe was a trek of forty-two miles, and it was accomplished in three days, which was good going for a burdened column over bad roads.

At Kahe we rested a day and marched at midnight on 22nd-23rd May. The column was now trekking through bush and following the course of the Pangani River, about a quarter of a mile east of its banks. Thus, we hold well west of the Usambara Railway, but are travelling parallel to it. This is a sound manoeuvre, for our position here will always worry the enemy in front of our forces operating on, or near, the railway in conjunction with us. It is clearly seen that, should the enemy on the railway make a stand, they would at once be threatened with a flank or rear movement from this side, unless they had sufficient forces to oppose, and hold, both columns. The country through which we are passing is flat, and mostly grown with thorn bush. There are no hills, excepting the distant ranges far out on our right and left. The soil here is sandy, and sometimes lava-strewn. Signs of game are plentiful. The column marched for ten hours before, in the forenoon of the following day, halt was called, and we camped. All were tired out, for, under any circumstances, a night march is trying; but we had been losing sleep for some days now, and were feeling strained accordingly. Regarding night marching, it is extraordinary how difficult it becomes to keep awake, either marching or on horseback, when monotonously plodding along. Commonly you will see a man dozing on his feet, but marching unsteadily on, and if the man in front of him should have occasion to halt, the sleeping man behind will walk forcibly into him, as an unseeing pedestrian may bump into a lamp-post.

During the early morning, on today's march, an astonishing incident occurred. Some of us, on the transport line, were suddenly startled by the rush of an animal from the bush, and were amazed to witness a buck jump clean across the road, over the top of a double line of mules. Half a dozen white men and some natives saw this almost unbelievable feat. The buck landed on the far side of the road only two yards away from me, and I think it was a hartebeest, but in the half-light I was unable to be quite certain of the species.

The following day, though we started at 3 a.m., the column had only got forward about eight miles when halt was called in the evening. Heavy bush had been encountered and was responsible for our slow progress, for laboriously a roadway had to be cut before the column could pass onwards. After camp was established, working parties went out ahead to continue hacking a clear way onward. About midnight we loaded our transport up, and moved out on the march about 3 a.m. We trekked all day slowly forward, and did not camp until after dark. It was a long, hard day, and everyone is feeling the pinch of meagre rations and want of sleep. The trail, being obstructed by heavy bush, continued bad, until in the afternoon the column emerged into an open grass-grown valley and made headway thenceforward smoothly and rapidly. Today we have passed well beyond, and outflanked, Lembeni, on the railway—the point at which the German forces congregated on retiring from Kahe. Apparently the enemy have cleared.

The following day, the 26th of May, the column did not trek until 1 p.m., so that all, thank God, had the opportunity of securing a complete night's sleep. Much refreshed and more cheerful was the column that marched out today. Late in the evening we camped near the Pangani River, about op-

ADVANCE FROM FRONTIER TO MOROGORO

Scale 1:1,200,000.

Miles

Railways
Roads
Column Advance
Enemy Engaged

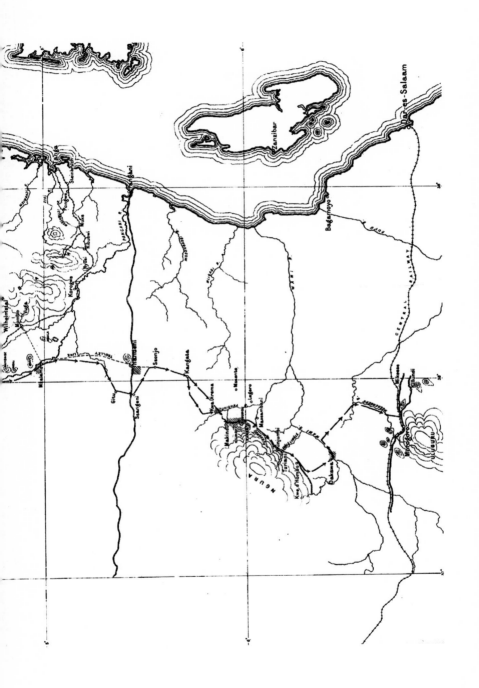

posite Same Station, which lay away to the east of us on the railway. The weather continues rainless, and very hot.

27th May—Trekked all day—a hot and wearisome march. The country we passed through was level and open, and we pushed, on rapidly. The enemy are apparently, fleeing far, for no resistance has been encountered, and our pace is accordingly as fast as man and beast can stand. Last night, ten Askaris and one white were captured in a patrol encounter.

28th May—This Sunday morning we were astir at 3 a.m. and trekked until the late afternoon. The pace, and the heat, and the lack of water between camps are beginning to wear down the endurance of man and animal. The men were very tired, and cheerless, when they reached camp today; they had been loaded with equipment and on their feet for thirteen hours, and were almost past exerting themselves to cook food and look after their odd accoutrements. The oxen and mules, too, were about *all in* ere they reached the end of today's trek, and the poor brutes, who must needs endure all in dumb suffering, get little enough care when the men who look after them are so very tired out at the end of such a day as this. Still passing through good game country. One herd of buffalo and many zebra were seen today.

29th May—At 4 a.m. loaded up transport ready to march, but did not move off until two hours later. No rations this morning ; supplies are stuck on the road behind When the battalion marched out I received orders to stay back in camp to try to secure rations. This was accomplished during the forenoon, and I then proceeded forward with three food-loaded carts drawn by poor jaded oxen that were very far gone—during the drive forward two completely exhausted oxen had to be turned loose and a make-shift arranged by lightening one cart and driving it with a single span of oxen.

Meantime the enemy had been shelling the column ahead with one of their 4·1 naval guns, in position on the

South Pare
Mountains.

Railway
to Tanga.

The Neck at "German Bridge": Engagement 30th May, 1916.

railway. When I approached the column, they were halted in extended formation in the bush. Before reaching them I had to cross an extensive open sand-flat where the carts raised a cloud of dust, and this caught the enemy's eye, for suddenly their gun—which had ceased firing for a space—boomed forth, and their shells, one by one, whizzed wickedly in close proximity. Some fifteen to twenty shells were sent at us before we had crossed that open space, but none found the mark, though three of them landed, straight in the centre of the trek, uncomfortably close in front. When we got through, it amused us to think that those innocent old carts had drawn the enemy's fire—perhaps we were mistaken for artillery, or the dust-cloud of moving troops. On joining the battalion there was general rejoicing at the sight of rations, and something to eat was issued forthwith. About sunset the column drew off to the right, and camped near the river. Today, instead of heading south as usual, we have followed the river-course almost due east, and have approached close to the railway and the South Pare Mountains. The advance troops of our column are today in touch with the enemy. We have been placed with the reserve force and remain in readiness close behind. The enemy's position is at the entrance, of the narrow neck formed by the meeting of the Pangani River and the hills at the south end of the Pare Mountains. Through this narrow fairway goes the Usambara Railway on its route to Tanga.

Next day, 30th May, the troops in front, under General Sheppard, attacked the enemy positions across the neck, and fighting continued throughout the day; the 2nd Rhodesians bearing the brunt of the battle. Close on darkness the enemy force retired, and escaped overnight. Casualties were fairly severe on both sides, for the fighting was stubborn, and the enemy stuck gamely to their positions. While our column was thus attacking, the eastern column—on the railway—had, some distance back, gone over the Pare Mountains and closed in on Buiko from the eastern side of the range, thus threatening to surround the enemy, in the neck, if they should determine to hold on there.

Meantime, everyone in reserve, though keenly disappointed not to be called into the fight, made the most of a halt that was needed by all, while starving oxen and mules were fully watered, and turned loose to graze on the scant grass and low woody shrubs which grew on the ill-nourished sandy surface in the somewhat open bush.

No fires were permissible, since smoke might give our position away, and draw artillery fire or a night attack; and accordingly our grub consisted of *straight* bully and biscuit, and water, a fare we were very familiar with now.

In the small hours of the following morning we loaded up the wagons and pack-mules, and moved out again. But we did not go any considerable distance before halt was called on the battle-ground of yesterday. The battalion to which I belonged was then ordered ahead, but the transport remained behind, and I with it, much to my disgust—we were very keen in those days, and no one liked to miss the smallest chance of a fight.

While in camp I looked over the enemy's positions of yesterday. The entrenchments were all newly dug, and a splendid bridge was half constructed over the Pangani River. Apparently this was to have become a very strong position had time been allowed for its completion, and here we realised the wisdom of our forced marching. General Smuts in pressing on is giving the enemy little time to rest, and prepare for our oncoming. We have marched 145 miles, from Mbuyuni to Buiko, in the past thirteen days, and, since leaving Kahe, have had to break trail through uninhabited country, most of it standing thorn-bush forest. And, so that one may realise the extreme length of our day, I have been particular in recording the hours at which we started out on those treks. It will be seen that sometimes we trekked all night, sometimes we started at midnight, but most often it was a case of getting up at 2 a.m. or 3 a.m., or 4 a.m. in the cold, chill night, and away soon after.

However, our arrival at Buiko next day marked a pause in operations, for we were destined to remain in that locality for the next eight days, while the German railway was being repaired to this point, and our insufficient supplies were augmented.

The enemy had passed on through Buiko in their flight, and it was unoccupied by either them or civilian inhabitants. It was a small station composed of a few stone-built houses with cactus-fenced compounds, but with an extensive railway siding, and siding sheds. After resting here four days, the battalion crossed the Pangani River, opposite Buiko, by pontoon bridge, and were then employed in cutting a road, through dense bush, back north to the almost completed *German Bridge* at the entrance to *the neck*.

Where the open valley grass—which stretched north and south, following the river's course— joined with the rugged edge of the bush, we had pitched camp, and it was here that, short of rations, a comrade and I ventured to hunt for meat for the pot.

It was about 4.30 on the second morning in camp. I turned over luxuriously in my blankets, and lay on my back blinking hazily at the overhead stars. It was within that dreamless hour before rising time, when the many disturbances of night on war service had passed away, and given place to peaceful rest and deep, delicious comfort and content. Half consciously I saw that dawn was breaking, and was aware that overnight I had promised to go on a surreptitious game hunt at daylight. What a fool's promise I thought that now! And I nestled snugly into the blankets for just "five minutes more."

"Buck! Come on!"

Rudely I was startled to active wakefulness, as the words of Lieutenant Gilham broke into my slumbers in a low voice.

"Right!" I called back as I sat upright. It was full daylight. Gilham was pulling his boots on in his lair under a bush a few yards away. We grinned at each other and dressed rapidly, silently; we knew the value of stealth.

Rations were low. Flour, and half a pound of bully beef, had been yesterday's issue, and Gilham, a veteran from South Africa, had come to me with the scheme to clear into the bush at daylight on the morrow. It was against orders to shoot, and perhaps against orders to leave the camp, but, being old hunters, and hungry, the old instinct got the better of discipline, and we had agreed to *chance it* in the morning.

All ready! Gilham lit a cigarette—that was in the days when we still had a few—lifted a service rifle, and started off, with a nod to me to come on. Signing to my black boy, Hamisi, I followed out, between the line of sleeping trek-tired soldiers, who lay along the west front of our perimeter. Immediately we were in the dense thorn-bush and wending our way laboriously, carefully, westward through the cruel-fanged jungle of countless cactus needles and grasping hook-thorns. It was the familiar type of African bush—dry, waterless, gravel and sand surface, grown with low wide-branching thorn-trees at fairly open intervals, filled in with a dense undergrowth of smaller shrubs, sisal, cactus, and grasses, until only narrow sand washes, or game paths, remain open, for short intervals, here and there. Through this one wends his way, zigzagging, dodging, stooping, and always on the look-out to move along the line of least resistance.

It is rough going, as rough as one will meet with in many travels. If one who has not experienced it can think of a hard mountain climb, or of a long march at the end of twenty miles, or of stiff canoe-going up-river, one may realise something of the stress of endurance. For the rest—the scratching, patience-trying obstacles—if you would picture the worst of them—the thorn-tree *mgoonga*— imagine half a dozen groups of Stewart tackle clutching along your arm or leg or helmet, while another lot threatens to tear your shirt back to rags. When you are hooked, you cannot free yourself by forcing forward; you must draw gingerly back, and extricate each barb with commendable patience; be impatient, and you will instantly be hooked up worse than ever. I will carry memories of *mgoonga* as long as I live. But the bush is not all dense, and this morning, after an hour's travelling, we found more open spaces, along which one could sometimes look to right or left or in front, for fifty yards or so. We were then well out from camp, and, with a cross wind from the south aiding us, we judged we could safely fire our rifles without fear of sound of report reaching back to head-quarters.

In whispers we agreed "all clear," and the locks of our rifles clicked, as cartridges were slipped into place, ready for action, while the boy dropped fifty yards behind, as we moved ahead in Indian file, silently, alertly, Gilham leading. We were hungry, and we meant to have meat!

We had not gone more than half a mile, when suddenly a single buck jumped from behind a bush, close in, and showed for an instant, in full view, as it bounded behind the cover of the jungle. One breathless instant, and it was gone, untouched. There had been no time to shoot, though we had seen enough to name it a *Lesser Koodoo* doe, a delicate, graceful thing, near to the size of a red deer, with prominent widespread ears. Eagerly we had realised the valued prize; keenly we realised it had vanished—alarmed, and impossible to follow. In undertone I *swore*, and Gilham muttered "bad luck," each in mind appraising the venison's goodly proportions, and hungry friends waiting rations in camp. Regrets were vain. More keen than ever, we moved, on again, the actual sight of game whetting our appetite for a kill. But no! The fates were unkind. At the end of two miles of careful stalking we halted, and had not fired a shot. Spoor in plenty had been encountered, principally the sharp-pointed sand-print of impala hoofs or the untidy scraping and burrowing of a family of wart hog. Many were fresh tracks, and promised the momentary appearance of game, but the shadow of the bush held motionless and lifeless, blank cover from which the treasures we sought had travelled   at first suspicion of danger's footfall. Twice we had flushed large flocks of guinea-fowl, magnificent birds and king of spoil for shot-gun in Africa; but, armed with rifles only, we were this day in mind to be impatient with the flutter and disturbance of their cackling, and heavy-winged rise from cover, when we rudely chanced in upon their morning breakfasting. And so, as duty demanded our presence in camp at 9 a.m., we were halted at the turning-point—empty-handed and disconsolate. Gilham wasn't saying much. He never did when hunting, but one might judge he was mourning his luck, as none too gently he rolled an uncouth cigarette out of notepaper and rough-cut Boer tobacco. While he smoked, we decided to circle up-wind, southward to begin with, and then, when clear of our outbound line, to strike for camp over fresh ground.

We were soon off again. The sun was now up and be-ginning to make itself felt in the bush. In an hour it would be stifling hot in those enclosed surroundings. We had not gone far—a half-mile or so—and we were crossing some open bush—abreast in open order—when a low whistle from Gilham, on my right, warned me to halt my cautious walk abruptly. He was not in view, but I caught the movement of his rifle rising, and almost instantly the report followed. Fifty yards ahead a buck jumped from behind a bush and stood face on, startled; fearful astonishment and bewilderment ap-parently making it unable to run for its life. Hurriedly, too hurriedly! I fired—and missed to the left, and off went our quarry bounding through the bush, we following at a run, not certain the animal was unscathed, and hoping it might be wounded. But the buck had vanished, and no sight of blood rewarded an inspection of his tracks. We had missed. Fools we felt, and deserved our self-condemnation—too keen! Over-anxious! the certain temperament to make even the old hand miss *a sure thing*. The buck had attracted my notice. During our fourteen months of patrolling the German-East-British-East frontier I had not seen its kind before. It was a buck like an impala antelope, but it stood slightly taller, and was of extremely delicate build, while the neck was noticeably very long and very slender; the horns curved back, as with the buck impala, but were more closely set together than with that species. Gilham named it a *Gerenuk* antelope.

Again we moved on, and by and by drew near to the distance from camp where we dare not fire. Suddenly a shot rang out, again from Gilham, on my right. I could neither see him nor his object as the bush was dense, and I paused anxiously. A moment, and a cheery shout rang out—"All right, come on!" and I hurried over to find my partner proudly surveying a prostrate *Gerenuk* doe, for, strangely enough, it was again this novel species which Gilham had spotted and dropped with a bullet high in the shoulder. It was a beautiful beast, though a doe, killed by fate of the pot-hunter's need, slender and delightfully delicate of build, with a coat of close, short, glossy hair, dark chocolate brown, above the central sides, where a distinctive horizontal line clearly separated the darker upper parts from those a shade or two lighter below. Many were our ejaculations of joy over our prize! Here was meat at last!—and venison!—fit reward for our strenuous stalk. Proudly now we would steal in upon our camp comrades and revel in a goodly feed all round. For one day at least bully beef would not plague our palate.

Without loss of time we cut the meat up, loaded the black boy, and, carrying the remainder ourselves, we set off for camp, deciding we were now too close in to shoot further.

Nearing camp, half an hour later, we put up at intervals, singly, numbers of dainty dodging Dik Dik, the smallest African antelope, which lairs and jumps off like a British hare, and which in size it barely exceeds. These little animals are usually sought with shot-guns, and give very tricky shooting. They are a much-prized table delicacy.

Our entrance to camp was a masterpiece of secret movement, and bush-cutting parade found us on duty outwardly severe but inwardly rejoicing over our morning's outing. And so had we a glimpse of sport in this famous big-game land while we passed on trek, keen on the trail of even bigger game.

On 9th June, the entire column—which had crossed the river from Buiko and had assembled at our bush camp on the previous day—again marched out on trek, and continued down the Pangani. In the late afternoon, the advanced troops at the head of the column engaged rear-guards of the enemy, and heavy fighting for a time ensued before the native village of Mkalamo. Our position then was about opposite Wilhelmstal and Mombo, two of the principal stations of the Usambara Railway.

On entering Mkalamo, next day, it was found to be a village composed of a few wrecked trading stores—burnt down by the enemy—and a large number of grass-built native *shambas*. Here an important light trolley-line, from Mombo, crossed the Pangani and passed through the village, and on into the bush where it. continues a course to Handeni, which is a town, some thirty miles farther south, on the broad trade road from the mouth of the Pangani into the interior. The fighting took place last evening a short distance north of the village, and the rear-guard action of the enemy was, apparently, solely to hold us off until darkness, for it is reported now that over 2,000 enemy were here yesterday, and that they evacuated the village and neighbourhood overnight. Rumours are persistent that the remainder of the Usambara line down to Tanga is almost completely clear of German forces, and that all enemy are now making for the Central Railway. The length of railway line from Mombo out to Tanga on the east coast is about seventy-five miles. It should greatly assist the forwarding of supplies if the port of Tanga and this section of railway fell into our hands; if it is not already seriously destroyed.

But it soon became evident that General Smuts intended to continue the pursuit south, toward the Central Railway, without waiting for the complete clearing of the remainder of the line.

We remained two days at Mkalamo, holding on while operations on the railway in this neighbourhood progressed. On 12th June we marched some six miles forward to the angle of the Pangani River where it changes direction and flows east to the sea, and there we again halted for a couple of days. Rations have been short for the past two weeks, and transport difficulties are evidently increasing behind. Moreover, most of the bridges on the railway from Moschi have been destroyed, or partly destroyed, by the enemy, so that there is delay in making use of any railway line, until hasty repairs are completed.

Regarding food we are limited at present to flour, and bully beef, and tea, and sugar, no bacon, no jam, no biscuit—and bare flour, without bacon fat or lard to cook it with, is almost a *straw* ration, for flour and water dropped into a dry canteen lid doesn't make anything digestible or palatable. But if one is hungry it is eaten, and really the men were wonderfully patient over their *dough-nuts*, and such scanty grub, even though they grew lean—for you know the popular old song beginning: "*What's the use of worrying?*" which is the never-dying axiom of our ever plucky soldiers. Being much in need of meat now, I went out hunting in the afternoon of both days, but without success. Many tracks of rhinoceros were crossed in this neighbourhood, but small game is apparently very scarce. Some day, in hunting in proximity to the enemy, I expect the game will be Germans instead of buck, but it's worth that risk of adventure, and if Germans are about in the bush, it's as well to know it.

15th June—Réveillé at 4 a.m., and soon after the column marched out. This morning we bid goodbye to the Pangani River, after having followed its course for 135 miles, and headed south in. the direction of the far-off Central Railway, and Morogoro—to reach which a great area of wilderness bush would have to be penetrated. Marched today over un-made dust-deep tracks, and camped in the bush at night after advancing some sixteen miles. Rations dwindling; flour, tea, and sugar only issued today.

The following day we continued onward, and, after completing some twelve miles, camped at 8 p.m., at Gitu, north-west of the considerable station of Handeni, on to which the eastern column was advancing. Rations today, ½lb. bully beef, coffee, and biscuits.

Next day the column continued onward into the south, and during the day emerged from wilderness bush into a country of plentiful small-croft cultivation—the first country of this kind that we have encountered since leaving Moschi. Native huts and mealie patches were on all sides amongst the bush, which is now fairly open and of fertile growth.

Toward noon we crossed the broad, well-made caravan road which comes from the coast station of Pangani, and runs far west into the interior. Soon after crossing this road we climbed into low hill country, and camped at Ssangeni, a na-tive village west of Handeni—some houses of which were now visible, about eight miles distant, at the foot of an iso-lated, prominent, cone-shaped *kopje*. Today's meagre rations, sugar (no tea), 1 lb. meat, and biscuits.

Sunday, 18th June—Lay all day in position occupied last night. South African troops went out from the column in the early morning under operation orders. Recent information as to the enemy's strength estimates that the force opposed to us, in the Handeni neighbourhood, is twelve companies of infan-try, two 4·1 naval guns, and fourteen maxim machine-guns.

19th June—In camp. Today the news reached us that Handeni had been occupied by General Sheppard's column, and also that the South Africans operating from our column

✶✶✶✶✶✶✶ Interims-Banknote ✶✶✶✶✶✶✶✶✶

Die

Deutsch-Ostafrikanische Bank

zahlt bei ihren Kassen im D. O. A. Schutzgebiet dem
Einlieferer dieser Banknote ohne Legitimationsprüfung

1   Eine Rupie   1

Daressalam/Tabora   Deutsch-Ostafrikanische Bank
1. Februar 1916.   Zweigniederlassung Daressalam

Gebucht von: In Vollmacht:

52137

Der Gegenwert dieser Banknote ist bei dem Kaiserlichen
Gouvernement von Deutsch-Ostafrika voll hinterlegt.

Kadri ya noti hii imewekwa sahihi katika Kaiser-
liches Gouvernement von Deutsch-Ostafrika

Wer Banknoten nachmacht oder verfälscht oder nach-
gemachte oder verfälschte sich verschafft und in Verkehr
bringt, wird mit Zuchthaus nicht unter 2 Jahren bestraft

52137

GERMAN PAPER RUPEE.

had engaged the enemy near here yesterday, and inflicted some casualties, but the enemy would not long stand their ground, and fought their familiar bush-covering retreating fight. To-day, from the native habitations, some food was collected by our hungry troops. My orderly obtained some welcome delicacies in the following strange manner: he bartered an old shirt for two chickens, an under-vest for seven eggs, and an old football sweater for six vegetable-marrows. Money held little inducement to the natives here; they were in great need of clothing, and it was apparel they sought. They say that sugar and clothes are finished in the German camps.

Crude, locally minted brass coins and printed paper one-rupee notes were plentiful among the natives, here and elsewhere. Those they have received from the Germans since war began in payment for food collected, by native consent or by force. If the war failed for the German this very doubtful currency would be unredeemable and valueless, and so the ignorant natives were warned that it was poor, if not totally false, this wealth which they held.

On the 20th and 21st of June we remained at Ssangeni. In the evening of the 20th advanced South African troops engaged the enemy ahead, and heavy conflict ensued, and lasted some two or three hours. Later, one of the returned wounded reported that the South African casualties were 15 killed and 75 wounded, and that the enemy had had some 200 casualties, but none of this information was authentic, though it was sufficient to show that a sharp encounter had taken place.

Next day, the 22nd of June, the column accomplished a long march forward, trekking on from 9 a.m. until 8 p.m., with but one hour halt, and camped, at the end of the day, at the native village of Kangata some twenty-five miles ahead of our last camp. It was a long, hot, trying day, and particularly wearisome when sheer exhaustion laid hold of the heavily burdened soldiers toward the evening of the day. On the march, the column passed through Ssonjo about noon, having travelled easterly across country on a native bush-path until the Handeni-Ssonjo road had been intersected. Our course thenceforth had been due south. The retreating enemy, falling back from Handeni, held up our advance by occasional sharp short-lived rear-guard actions—bursts of firing on the advance guard—and the country, which was bush-grown on either side of the narrow native road, was well suited to their hide, and strike, and run away manoeuvres.

A number of oxen and horses were left dead on the road-side today. No *feed* ration is available for issue to transport animals at present, and this unfortunate state of affairs is telling heavily on the live-stock. Our own rations have been somewhat better during the last three days.

On the 23rd of June rations of meat and flour were cooked before the column marched at 4 a.m. We were in for a long trek, and were told to expect a fight at the end of it. Our objective was the bridge-head, and the hills commanding it, where the bush-road crossed the Lukigura River, and where the enemy had dug in. The eastern column was, in conjunction, to advance down the narrow native road, which runs through the bush from Handeni to Makindu at the northern end of the populated   Nguru Mountains, while we were to circle away wide to the west and attack at the heart of the hill position. All night we trekked, excepting for one halt at midnight. It was slow, monotonous work for this column, which must have stretched to a sinuous length of miles; for it was necessary, on account of the density of bush and jungle growth, to feel the way along in single file, on a narrow native bush-path over which a native guide was leading us to our goal. Moving, then halting till the kink in the line straightened out, then on again, so dragged the night hours wearily on; and progress was made, though we travelled as sheep in a strange defile, led we knew not where. After midnight bitter cold set in and chilled our scanty shirt-clad bodies, and when dawn broke the red-hot sun was for once welcomed in Africa, as it warmed us to life again. But still, when the day dawned, the trekking column held onwards, and all through the day we marched, until 4.30 p.m.—and then to battle. I have never seen men more utterly tired and woebegone than our men at the time of their approach on Lukigura River. They had been marching twenty-four and a half hours, kit-laden and without substantial food; and yet, when they went into battle all fatigue was forgotten, or they were careless of further physical trial; and they fought like madmen—and as heroes.

It was for us a short, hot engagement, and the height and the village of Kwa-Direma were stormed at the point of the bayonet, and in our hands ere the fall of dusk. It transpired that the enemy had confined all their attention to the bush-road from Handeni, down which the eastern column was advancing, and they were taken completely by surprise when our attack pounced on them from the west, and inflicted complete defeat and heavy loss. Meantime the eastern column attacked below, on the road in the bush, east of Kwa-Direma, and carried the bridge-head over the Lukigura River, inflicting further punishment on the beaten enemy.

During the early part of the night our new positions on the hill-crest were shelled by the enemy's naval guns. A few casualties resulted, but most of the shells were high and went over the hill to burst in the vacant bush below.

The next few days were spent in camp at Kwa-Direma. Here I made some sketches of the position and neighbourhood for G.H.Q., and spent some time in the bush, much of which was breast-high in tangled undergrowth and rank grass, but which nevertheless showed traces of where the enemy had scattered and hidden at the time of our attack.

Here, one morning, my porters captured a small antelope—*Harvey's* duiker—even at the door of my native-erected grass hut, where it had rushed in fear and bewilderment on being disturbed near by.

Here, also, I had some practice with a 1-in. Krupp gun which we had captured in. the late engagement. Though completely out of date, it was a vicious and accurate little piece, and, as long as the captured ammunition lasts, it has been decided to have it added for service to the machine-gun section of which I am in charge. A day later, too, I took part in some tests of armoured-car armour plate, at the request of Major Sir John Willoughby. The armour plate withstood the blow of the Krupp gun shell at 100 yards range, and was merely dented. We then tested the German made-up iron-plate shield on the Krupp gun. Our service rifle failed to penetrate the plate, but a ·245 high-velocity sporting rifle of Sir John Willoughby's put a neat hole clean through it.

Sunday, 2nd July—And for once, as it rarely is on service, it has been a quiet day, and like a Christian "day of rest." And being a Sunday it recalls our homes, from which we are longing very much for news. Mails reach us at very long intervals of a month or more, and for weeks we have been hoping for home news. The column has lain a week at Kwa-Direma, and we are said to be waiting here until supplies come up in quantity. We have had no full ration since getting here, and we are all feeling the effect of the shortage. From two natives, whom I persuaded two days ago to go to their home in the hills to forage for food for me, I have today purchased, in exchange for old clothing, some mealie-meal flour and thirteen fowls. Great the rejoicing, for this is, in these bad days, a windfall for myself and some of the men. One hen, a white-plumaged one, I kept a few days, and by then it had proved so friendly and tame that I decided to spare its life and keep it as a pet. Thereafter, here and on trek, it caused much amusement and comment. It lived with me a few months before it was stolen by someone whose hunger overcame his scruples, and each day, whether on trek or in camp, it laid me an egg. Very peculiarly this hen learned to come to roost wherever

I lay, and, more curious still, it was never at a loss as to my whereabouts when released among the feet of hurrying soldiers in strange surroundings at the end of a trek. On trek she was generally tied down in a horse-bucket, and carried by my native servant.

The next few days passed uneventfully, except that much time was given over, on my part, to increasing the proficiency of the machine-gunners and to the training of mules, both old and new, to complete familiarity with their saddles and loads. Once during those days the camp was sniped at night, but in the darkness no damage was done.

On 7th July we loaded up and marched out south-west, on the bush-road over the Lukigura River. In the afternoon Makindu, which had already been occupied by General Sheppard's column, was reached, and there we camped. Immediately on camping we were shelled by the enemy for about an hour, but little damage was done.

Makindu, this village on the Msiha River, which we had reached and where we were destined to stay for a time, is still some seventy-five miles north of our objective—Morogoro, and the Central Railway. But a great trek has been accomplished, for we are now 260 miles from Mbuyuni, our starting-point on the frontier. Needless to say this exceedingly long line of communication has made the transport of supplies a tremendous undertaking, therefore it was not unreasonable that, for the next month, we lay at Makindu while transport difficulties were mastered and clearly organised, and the shorter line, in from Tanga by rail, was opened and brought to our assistance.

This long pause, too, was beneficial to the over-strained troops. Speaking of our own battalion, they were very far through in physique at the time we reached Makindu, and in numerical strength they were, all told, under 200 strong. True, they were "the flower of the flock" in endurance, this remnant of the 1,200 which sailed from England, but even they were withered, and withering, with long fight, on short commons, against unhealthy soul-exhausting climate. Nine officers remain who have gone through all since the beginning, including the doctor, the O.C., and the second-in-command.

At Makindu we had our first prolonged experience of shell-fire, for throughout our occupation of this place we were continually shelled by the enemy's naval guns, and sometimes suffered considerable loss. The enemy's fire was throughout particularly accurate, as if the camp were directly under observation from some undetected lookout in the high ranges of the Nguru Mountains, on our south-west—which, at some points, had an extreme elevation of some 6,100 feet. It was here seen that the native Africans were very nervous and fearful of shell-fire, and their raw instincts with difficulty stood the strain. It is a trying thing for anyone to wait idly inactive for a shell's vicious death-dealing on-coming, but it is much more trying to the half-wild senses of a black man than to a white man. We had no artillery with a range sufficient to reach the enemy's naval guns, so that the only retaliation on our part was accomplished by dropping bombs from our aeroplanes. As soon as the enemy ceased firing, invariably our 'planes went up, and, when over the German positions—cunningly though they were concealed in the bush—bombs were dropped on every likely target. It became amusing when the intention of the opposite foe became clear, this persistent blow for blow *strafe* between the enemy guns and our aircraft.

At Makindu two delayed mails were received, and great was the rejoicing; even though some of the letters were six months old.

It was at Makindu, too, that, one evening, my pet white hen, which had been with me since the fight at Lukigura River, killed a small snake 15 inches long. This I had never seen done before by domestic fowl. She was very timid and wary in pecking at the snake until very sure she had stricken it to death, where-after, with much exertion, she swallowed it whole as if it were a worm. She is indeed a funny old hen. Still she never gets lost amongst all the confusion of camp life, and each night she comes home, often after roaming far, to roost within a yard or two of me.

While at Makindu I did some reconnaissance and sketching for G.H.Q., and saw much of the bush country beyond the camp. The following notes of one such reconnaissance will serve to give an idea of its nature and the type of country.

Patrol undertaken to investigate country on east flank out to the track crossing from Massimbani to Legero, which is well behind the German position. Patrol left Makindu at 4 a.m. on the 1st of August, 1916, and returned to Makindu 3 p.m. on the 3rd of August, 1916. Our southerly direction, from point of setting out, was held on a bearing of 160 degrees throughout the advance to Massimbani track. The distance, reckoned by time, from starting-point to Massimbani track is about twelve miles. The distance to intermediate grass track crossing from Mssente to Ruhungu is about 4¼ miles. The first seven miles is good and fast-going for vehicle road through open forest—little forest cutting should be necessary, and no grading. The last five miles of the total distance passes through some parts of less open forest, and some timber felling will be necessary in places. In this locality a few narrow *islands* of dense bush—lying east and west—will be encountered, but these may always be evaded by keeping round their western extremities. No rivers, or soft riverbeds were encountered; throughout the surface soil is dry and hard. Where the Mssente track was crossed, the bearing on to the Ruhungu position was 260 degrees. Said bearing follows down an open grass valley which is unobstructed by forest and in full view of Ruhungu hills. The mountain range appeared close at the Mssente track, at most some two to four miles distant, but the range viewed from the Massimbani track appeared far off, and as if viewed from a lower level. By eye I judged the distance here to be eight to ten miles, and later, sketching out the course of the patrol, I find it to be 8½ miles. The impression given me, and this is borne out, was that in avoiding Massimbani village we were very wide of the hills and the enemy's line of communication to his positions in front. In regard to this I might state that, after crossing over the Mssente track about a mile, a bearing of 5 degrees to 7 degrees would draw in more closely to the mountain foot-hills, and might have better results. From the Massimbani track a long, fairly low range of hills was apparent in the distance, tailing off south beyond the prominent peak of Kanga (elevation 3,280 ft.). The Mssente track was a mere path in the grass and had no appearance of being much in use. The broad Massimbani track is apparently one of long standing, and had appearance of being much used by the enemy, though no movement was observed while for some hours we lay hidden on watch. There was no telephone line on the Massimbani track.

On the return journey the patrol held slightly easterly until, after going three miles, the Lukigura River was struck. The course of the river was then followed for about 2½ miles. Kwa-Beku, where shown on field map, was not observed. *Kraals* were seen on the opposite side of a lagoon on the river, after we had followed its course for about a mile, and signs of grazing cattle were noticed near here, but the huts across the river appeared uninhabited. The route by the course of the Lukigura River is obstructed by dense patches of jungle, and the going is bad. If it were necessary to approach the river for purpose of securing water for animals and troops, I would state that a short distance north of the Massimbani track, say two miles, the open forest runs out to the river-bank and access to water could here be easily accomplished.

Such was a manner of unravelling the mystery of the important and unknown details of the map in this ever new and strange country.

5th August, 1916—At 3.30 a.m. the camp was astir—today we were to march, today we were again to begin active operations. After great overnight operations, this morning we trekked out from Makindu on the road back to Kwa-Direma, for it transpired that we were, as Divisional Reserve, to take part in an encircling right flank movement through the Nguru Mountains between the main block of hills and the Kanga-Kilindi range, on the eastern side of which the enemy stronghold sheltered. Arriving at Kwa-Direma about midday, we found a large concentration of forces there composing General Hannyngton's Brigade and part of the Divisional Reserve. Previous to our arrival mounted South African troops under General Brits had already left to commence the advance through the hills.

The following two days I have no wish to recall, but that they are necessary to this narrative. We began, and laboured incessantly to advance our column of troops and transport into hill country that proved to be quite impassable, for any but unburdened man or beast, owing to its succession of deep valley bottoms and steep untracked hills. But nevertheless we laboured on for two days, on such strenuous work as cutting roads through forest, laying corduroy logging over swamp marsh, and, at the hills, in-spanning two to three complete teams of mules or oxen to drag each wagon with excessive effort up the stupendous grades. At the end of the second day, after we had in all covered some eight to ten miles, the project was abandoned, and we received orders to return the way we had come.

Next day we again reached Kwa-Direma, and none were sorry to be out of those hills. Meantime the operations that had been going on, on both flanks, with a view to attacking or surrounding the Ruhungu positions unaccountably failed to get to grips with the enemy, who, probably in fear of a rear attack, succeeded in secretly evacuating their stronghold while the mounted troops were working their way through the hills. This was to all a big disappointment, but the extremely awkward nature of the country proved again the enemy's disconcerting ally and for him his saving. This operation was, perhaps, meant to be our greatest effort to force a decision—at least so did we, at the time, regard it.

On the 9th of August we were back in Makindu, and on the 10th we proceeded along the road toward the Ruhungu position. Soon we found the road completely blocked by great trees that had been felled across it by the enemy, and in some places the road was also mined. Slowly we went forward throughout the day, investigating the level bush and the hillsides as we went. Once about fifty enemy were sighted, and lost again in the bush. Once a mounted patrol of sepoys fell in with the enemy, who surprised them when dismounted, and they lost their horses, and then their heads, while an advancing line of our men raked the bush with rifle-fire beyond them. Next day those horses, six of them, were found running free in the bush, and were caught and returned to their owners, one or two of them suffering from bullet wounds.

In the late afternoon we built a *boma* (bush fence) protection and camped for the night on the road; and again moved forward in the morning into the Ruhungu position. Progress was slow while the position, which was a very strong one in its systematic completeness, was carefully investigated, covered by machine-guns trained on the hill-slopes ahead. The position was completely occupied at 11 a.m. and all reported clear.

Going over the position I was astonished at the work that had been spent on it. For instance, on the low ground at the position defending the road, a wide carpet of sharply pointed, dangerous-looking, hand-cut pegs had been staked out in front of the whole trench line to protect it, apparently, from cavalry charge. This original and ingenious *entanglement* could not have been constructed without many, many days of labour by many men. Then, too, in the hills above, regular subterranean caves, and pits, had been excavated everywhere for protection from the attacks of our aeroplanes, some of them even hewn out of the solid rock by the industry of many hands.

In the afternoon we passed beyond Ruhungu, and in the evening camped by a small rivulet in low country east of the high Kanga Mountain top. Many small bush-log culverts on the road have here been destroyed by the enemy as they retired, and this has left the road impassable for transport until repairs are made.

The following day we advanced until the Russongo River was reached, and then camped, while working parties busily constructed a new bridge over the river.

At early dawn of the next day, which was Sunday the 13th of August, we trekked again onward through tree-covered hill country, and made a long march in a south-westerly direction, camping in the afternoon at Kinjumbi on the Luale Liwale River. The timber bridges destroyed, over streamlets and rivers, coursing numerously from the mountain watersheds, are now everywhere being roughly and speedily repaired, and the forces are hurrying forward in the wake of the escaping enemy. General Smuts is himself here today and hustling things forward.

Worked all through the night repairing the bridge over the deep-banked Luale Liwale River; then off over the river in the morning and onward, until again held up at Turiani, before which flows the large River Mwúhe, where two bridges had been blown up to block our passage. We have now descended into low, unhealthy marsh country, where the atmosphere is close and damp, and fly-ridden. For the remainder of the day and the next two days, swarms of us, like busy ants, laboured to and fro on the construction of the large timber-buttressed bridge being thrown across the high-banked river. At the end of the latter day fever laid hold of me, and left me with just enough energy doggedly to carry on. Toward evening, too, of the latter day the work drew to a close, and we marched out forthwith, at 7 p.m., to camp about midnight at Kwe d'Hombo.

Meantime the forces ahead had pushed on south to reach, on the 17th of August, the Wami River, there, at the bridge-head at the village of Dakawa, to enter into an all-day battle with the strongly entrenched enemy. The struggle was a fierce one, and again the enemy suffered severe punishment, but, nevertheless, they stubbornly defended their positions, on the opposite banks of the river, until night-fall, then to escape under cover of the screening darkness.

On the 19th, 20th, and 21st of August, I was employed going over and making plans of the Dakawa position, though still continuing a victim of vile malaria. This, however, was the last work I did for seven days, for I went hopelessly down with fever next day, and went into field hospital, while the force continued on, and on 26th August occupied Morogoro, and cut the Central Railway without meeting further enemy resistance.

I left ambulance quarters, and Dakawa, on the 28th of August, and reached Morogoro in the forenoon two days later, there to find that the battalion was still fifteen miles ahead. So, not to be done, I borrowed a mule and a broken-down German saddle, and caught up the column before night-fall, at Killundi, east of Morogoro on the low road south of the Central Railway. Over the country I had passed in coming from Dakawa great stretches of the bush grass had been burnt down by the enemy in their retirement, presumably so that there would not be even dry poor grazing for our already lean-flanked horses and cattle.

So we had reached Morogoro—which was a large, picturesque town below the northern foot-hills of the Ulugúru Mountains, with colonial well-built houses and bungalows, and palm-shaded, sand-carpeted streets, wherein moved native pedestrians in bright-coloured cotton garments swathed loosely over their shoulders and bodies. And here I must halt; though the columns halted not, and relentlessly continued their pursuit of the fleeing enemy. To reach Morogoro we had trekked some 355 miles, and in attaining our objective had

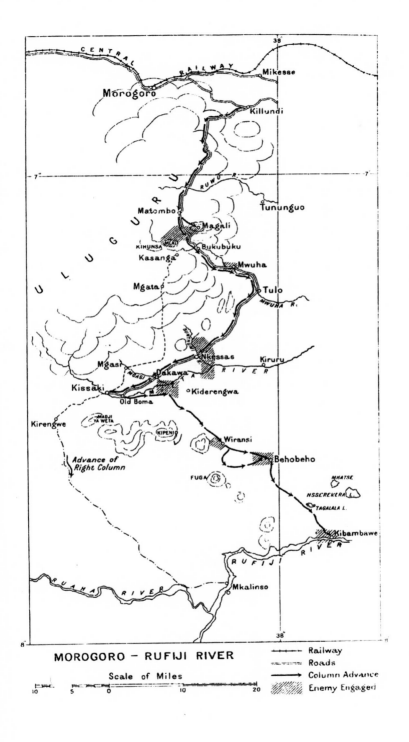

MOROGORO – RUFIJI RIVER

Scale of Miles

	Railway
	Roads
	Column Advance
	Enemy Engaged

taken part in the fall of the entire Central Railway; for in conjunction with our operation, and almost simultaneously, naval forces captured the port of Bagomayo, near Dar-es-Salaam; General Van Deventer's column cut the railway at Kilossa and Mpapua—over 100 miles west of Morogoro—while the Belgian forces, from the Congo, threatened and eventually captured Tabora—the interior terminal of the railway.

A few days later news came through that Dar-es-Salaam, the capital and chief port of the Protectorate, had surrendered to naval forces on the 4th of September.

After wrecking all the important steel-constructed bridges, and all the rolling stock on the railway, the enemy had now fled to the south into the only country that remained free to them—even though it was, beyond the Ulugúru Mountains, a country of bush and swamp and wilderness to which they fled, and entailed their final irrevocable departure from the last of their civilised settlements and trade-centres, and from their all-important railway.

Indeed, at this stage, it must have been patent to most of them that, in suffering this disaster, their country was lost; prolong the final capitulation though they may.

Chapter 6

The Third Stage

This was to be an advance less in ultimate distance than those previously undertaken, and accomplished, but proved to be through country much more attractive, in its early stages, yet, in its latter stages, more unhealthy and trying than anything we had so far experienced. The operations began in the very mountainous and beautiful Ulugúru mountains, south of Morogoro, mountains which were cultivated and habited by large numbers of natives, and which were rich in crop and pasturage and water, and truly the first fair country we had seen—if we except the Moschi area—that was not barren of almost everything but bush and wilderness. But thereafter, when we cleared those mountains, we bade good-bye to the last of fair scene and entered, for the remainder of the trek, the low-lying, unhealthy bush country that stretches like a great unruffled carpet right away to the banks of the Rufiji River, and beyond.

Our object was, first, to follow the enemy, and, secondly, to clear all the country north of the Rufiji River of enemy. To reach the Rufiji River from Morogoro was a trek in all of some 130 miles, the first fifty-five miles of which was through mountainous country. To clear the hills our column was to proceed through them on the east of the highest range; some ten miles east of us the eastern column was to work along parallel south-going tracks while a column composed entirely of South African troops, in co-operation, was to work down the country, west of the mountains, to close ultimately on the Fort of Kissaki.

Setting out on the 31st of August we trekked to begin with on a good *made* road, cut through the hills, and free of impossible grades, and encountered no opposition until we had got beyond Matombo village and mission station.

Meantime, in continuing without halt to follow the enemy from Morogoro, we were adding to supply difficulties, and saw little prospect of full rations in the near future. At Killundi, one day's march from Morogoro, no rations reached us, and the battalion in their need had a much-wasted trek-ox killed, and issued as emergency ration. Otherwise we had to make shift as best we could, and were hard put to it to assuage our hunger. A few small things were gathered from the neighbourhood, such as sugar-cane stalks to chew at, a few *paw-paws* (papaya), and wild tomatoes, a chicken or two; and one great find, a grey-marked goat from the hills.

On the 3rd of September we encamped at Ruwu River, an enemy encampment far down in a beautiful valley into which we had descended on a zigzag, well-engineered road cut out of the steep hill-sides in pre-war days at the expense of gigantic labour. The existence of this road through the hills was unknown to our command until the enemy retired by it from Morogoro. Fine tropical trees, on either side of the road, were tall and dark-foliaged and majestic, and the undergrowth luxuriant and flower-lit, while through the trees, every now and then, one glimpsed the fair valley and hills below and beyond. Everyone was filled with admiration for the beauties of the scenes we encountered on the final day of our march to Ruwu River, It was indeed very beautiful country!

The wide-spanned bridge over the river had been destroyed, but though the river was wide at this season it was shallow and not more than waist-deep, and the troops and the transport laboriously and successfully forded the firm gravel and sand-bedded stream. The Germans had had stores at Ruwu River, and here, in their hasty flight—for the enemy had apparently just abandoned the place—large quantities of shells and grenades were found dumped in the river-bed.

On the *4th of September,* leaving all transport behind, we marched out at 6.30 a.m., and again trekked through lovely hill country, especially in the early part of the day, when the road ran along parallel to the river, we being then on a regular mountain pass cut in the precipitous hill-sides that fell abruptly to the broad, bank-forested river, flowing below us on our right. The pass was a cutting that worked a way round to open country, penetrating, in its course, the great base of a mountain spur that abutted on to the very river-bank. In two or three places large boulders and rocks had been blown out of the upper side of the pass from perpendicular rock cliffs, and effectually blocked the way for all but nimble-footed men and mules. It was, though strange and very beautiful, a dangerous bit of road, and difficult, and would give our engineers and pioneers a very considerable task to make it again passable for transport. However, bad though the road was, the marvel was that the enemy had not completely blocked the way, for a few sticks of dynamite, well placed, could so easily have accomplished that purpose. It proved perhaps again that the enemy was hard pressed and flustered. During the morning the pass was negotiated, and we proceeded along a good road. After the column had passed Matombo village, the battalion received orders to occupy Magali Ridge—a high, long-backed hill off the road, on the left flank. This entailed a long five-mile drag up steep hill-sides, on narrow native foot-paths, that were awkwardly rutted and bouldered. However, by 4 p.m. we had laboured to the crest, and took up position for the night there.

Meantime, the Gold Coast Regiment—who had been landed at Dar-es-Salaam to augment our forces on this trek—

engaged the enemy on the right of the road in open, tree-clear hill country. This engagement, which continued on through the next two days, was like open guerilla warfare, and different therefore from all previous encounters which had taken place in thick bush country. We, from our high position—as all was quiet on this flank except for one short encounter—watched the fortunes of battle of our friends across the valley. Artillery was in action on both sides, and the white puffs of smoke told us plainly where the flying shells burst, and where the opposing forces were located, and holding on.

Gallantly the Gold Coast blacks, led by British officers, fought the blacks of the country, and steadily they dislodged them out of bush-patches, and from behind rocks, to drive them, bit by bit, up the many hill-slopes toward the Kihunsa Ridge; behind which lay the track to Mgata, and their second road of retreat to the south through Tulo or Kissaki.

Meantime, on our flank, as I have said, all was quiet except for one short *dust-up*. This was when, on the evening of the 5th, on a prominent knoll on the opposite ridge, south of Magali ridge, we discovered and destroyed, with mountain battery and machine-gun fire, the enemy's observation post which had been directing the fire of their naval guns—long-range guns—which shelled from positions some six miles in rear, and which our artillery could not attempt to reach, for at best ours were light pieces which had been got through the part-blocked pass at Ruwu River. As soon as this vital observation post was wiped out, the enemy's guns ceased fire, for there, far forward of the guns, had hidden the eyes that saw all—eyes that scanned the whole countryside, and the road, with the intentness of a bird of prey—and there had been the cunning hand on the wires of the telephone that told off every pulse-beat of the booming guns.

On the evening of the 6th the troops on the right flank had worked far out and up to the main ridge crest—some had even gone over it, in pursuit of fleeing enemy—and, on

114

the approach of dusk, the firing died down altogether and fighting ceased. Natives whom I questioned, who live in these hills, and have not deserted their homes in fear of approaching conflict, state that the force on the right flank is not the big one, but that the larger force is on the main road between here and Bukubuku, in which village, where a road joins in from the west, there is a large camp of enemy. On the last day of the fight the natives, who are extraordinarily quick in flashing news from hut to hut amongst their tribes, stated that all the enemy were preparing to leave the hills, and that they would go toward Kissaki Fort.

The 7th of September was a quiet day, and was spent in camp on the sun-hot ridge, while we grew impatient at our inactivity. Though all was quiet on our front, we could hear the battle call of big guns firing to the east, where the eastern column was *somewhere* in action.

8th September, 1916—Camp afoot at 4 a.m., and the battalion trekked at daylight; at that time commencing the descent from Magali ridge to the road, where we joined in with the column. About 10 a.m. we passed through Bukubuku, then deserted, but where large, carefully built barrack hutments extensively lined the road. This place had the aspect of being a large military centre, probably a training station for natives recruited from these populated hills. Late in the day, as we advanced steadily, the road began to wind down out of the hills until, to the south, there appeared before us a great level stretch of haze-softened bush country, reaching out as far as eye could follow. From noon onward, today, small but troublesome enemy rear-guards harassed our advance, until finally, in the evening, we drew in on larger forces and entered into a short engagement at Mwuha River and village. It promised, at one time, to be a hot set-to, but mountain-battery guns subjected the village to very heavy fire, and, when extended infantry proceeded to attack, the village was entered without noteworthy incident, for the enemy were found to be again retiring, and, as it was getting dark, we could not follow on their heels.

During the trek today quantities of abandoned stores were passed from time to time upon the road, principally field-gun ammunition, wagons, dump-barrows, and pioneering implements. We continue close on the heels of the enemy, and, fearful of standing up to our superior forces, they are apparently being hustled uncomfortably to get away each night, and must now be a much-harassed force.

Early next morning, when we moved out, we had not trekked far before we came on the enemy's rear-guard camp of last night, where some fires were yet kindled and freshly killed meat lay. about, quantities having been but partly used. Shortly after midday, the column marched into Tulo, which the enemy had hastily cleared from. Here, as at Bukubuku, were countless grass huts which had been built and used as barracks. The interiors of all were in disorder—rude furnishings, such as grass-laced couches and chairs, were upturned everywhere; mealie-meal flour, peas, beans, and paper lay scattered on the ground, or lay about in half-empty sacks against the walls, and all gave one the impression of a looted and abandoned camp, from which the occupants had fled in uncontrolled haste. An hour or two ago the enemy had been here—now they were fleeing through the bush and down the road leading south-west in the direction of Kissaki. Here, as at Ruwu, large quantities of shells and other ammunition were found dumped in the Mwuha River and abandoned. Besides the barrack huts already mentioned, there were the many native *kraals* of the permanent village of Tulo, and a number of these still contained their peaceful occupants. The following day, as I had lost a considerable number of machine-gun carriers, I recruited, for temporary service, twenty-one sturdy, ragged-garbed, almost naked natives from amongst the inhabitants of the village. These natives appeared friendly and willing to serve under us, although we had been but a few hours their masters. In their own dull way I suppose they reasoned that we were a great and powerful people, since we were driving their late masters before us.

The next four days we remained in reserve at Tulo, while the column went ahead to Nkessa's village, some thirteen miles farther on, on the Dunthumi River, and entered on an extensive encounter on a wide front.

My diary entries at this time again record great food shortage, and declare that the men have not enough food to keep together their sorely tried, used-up systems. And this was really so. Daily the ambulances took in men we lost on the march from sickness and *exhaustion*.

Being short of food at Tulo, and as the conditions did not improve, on the third and fourth day I went out to hunt for the pot, and, as we were now on the border of a large German game reserve, I found game plentiful, and shot five antelope, three reed-buck, and two impala. Other officers did likewise, and soon there was no shortage of buck meat in the, camp.

Meantime, during the 10th, 11th, 12th, and 13th of September, a stern struggle had been raging at Nkessa's, and not until the evening of the 13th were the enemy dislodged from their many positions and driven back some three miles south, and the hills and the river and the village occupied.

The day following I went forward to make a sketch survey of the battle-field, which, owing to the extensiveness of the operations, I did not complete until four and a half days later throughout that time labouring from daylight to dusk to get over the many positions. While I was at Nkessa's enemy movements were fairly quiet, excepting for some night shooting on 15th, 16th, and 18th. The enemy were entrenched across the Mgeta River about three and a half miles south of Nkessa's, and some of our forces were dug-in opposite them. For, for reasons beyond my knowledge, operations, and the active chase, had, for the time being, come to an end.

I give here a description of the country held by the enemy before Nkessa's village: to advance to the encounter Nkessa's was approached from the east on the Tulo-Kissaki road—a narrow, inferior road through the low country, and running westerly parallel with the southern foothills of the Ulugúru mountains, which were always visible well off to our right. The road throughout was over level grade, and passed through country of thorn-bush growth and tall, dense grass.

Approaching Nkessa's, the foothills draw in to close proximity of the village, and, about 2,100 yards north of the road, a prominent bush-covered hill, and a long ridge trending west, rise to an elevation of about 300 feet from dense, bush-grown bases, and command the flat country south and east; over which our forces advanced to attack.

South of the prominent hill, between the hill base and the road, the low ground formation is irregular, with small nullahs and mounds and the whole surface a dense tangle of bush growth and tall grass.

Adjoining this, and continuing to the eastern edge of the village, there is a square-planned rubber plantation, while above the northern boundary of it there is a low spur, on which is situated a group of planters' buildings. From those buildings, which are clearly in view from the low ground, a narrow road runs down, between the village boundary and the plantation, to the main road.

Across the main road, opposite the rubber plantation and the low ground below the hills, there is a large level mealie-field, clear of crop, which parallels the road for 1,000 yards or so from the village, and which has a narrow width at the village, but which opens out fan-wise to a depth of 550 yards at its easterly extremity, where it is bordered by a cotton-field in crop. East of the cotton-field, where some of our forces dug in, the country is level, with a surface of tall rank grass and a few bushes.

Bordering the south margin of the mealie-field, and continuing some distance east, is a belt of dark jungle composed of tall trees and tangled bush.

Immediately south of the tree belt, at the south-west margin, there is a village of native *kraals* hidden by some fields of tall-stalked mealies and by the tall, rank grass common to the low ground of the Dunthumi River, which in the rains is flooded.

Farther south of this there are no decided landmarks, the country running out like prairie, low and level, and grown with tall, rank grass, and screening the Dunthumi River, which swings on to an easterly course after it has left the hills and passed through Nkessa's village and beyond about a mile.

Turning now from the south aspect to the west aspect: immediately west of the prominent hill above the road, there runs north and south, across a deep parallel valley, a long ridge which, at its southern extremity, descends abruptly to the Dunthumi River, and from the ridge the course of the river is clearly seen below, in the immediate foreground, and running out south through its margins of tall grass. Across the river, and just north of the village, the country rises brokenly into low, bush-covered foothills. Those foothills were unoccupied by enemy. From the ridge Nkessa's village is not seen, it being under cover of the large mango trees, and palms, and thick forest, amidst which it is situated. However, it is a large village of native huts, with a broad white road running through the centre of it which is shaded with avenues of great densely leafed mango trees, and lined on either side with native dwellings, grass-thatched, mud-walled, sand-floored.

From the village, a track runs out south along the west bank of the Dunthumi River. The track is narrow but level, and passes through low country with the usual perplexing growth of tall, rank grass and thorn bush.

One may gather, from this detailed description, the immense natural difficulties of the country, and how hard it may be to turn an enemy out of such positions. Here the only area of open space—viz. the mealie-field—down which an attacking force might push rapidly forward, was ruthlessly exposed to enemy fire from no less than three sides—from the village, from the low bush north of the road, and from the dark tree-belt south of the road. It meant death to too many to attempt it. The alternative attack was to advance slowly, through the all-screening, hampering bush, upon those concealed entrenchments in the grass; never sure, even when the enemy are located by their fire, of the exact position of the foe; never sure, at any time, what the next twenty yards of jungle hold in store for you. You are blind from the time you enter the rank jungle growth until you reach the enemy's position, and you are lucky if at the end you have sighted an enemy at all, though you have been blazing away at one another at some fifty yards. And picture the difficulty of keeping in touch with your own people in such jungle, which, the moment you enter it, swallows you up in its depth of undergrowth as if you were a rabbit taking cover in a field of ripe corn. Not only is it difficult—I might say impossible, sometimes—to know where your own people are, who are advancing on the right or left, but also it is difficult to know the movements of the enemy. One moment they may be in front of you; a few moments more, and they may be gone, undetected—all but a few bluffing rifles—to a new position, or may be working round on an open flank.

Truly the enemy chooses his positions well, and it is the country, not he, well though he fights, that robs us again and again of decisive battle. Their positions are, with rare exceptions, chosen where they and their movements cannot be seen, and thus their strength, at the many points of battle, may be either a handful of men or a dozen companies. Moreover, under cover of the bush, their lines are flexible to any change, while always, in the rear, they have sure and safe lines of retreat by which they can escape in the bush, in a dozen directions, to meet again at a given point when their flight is over.

Moreover, the enemy is always on his own soil, whereas each new battle-front is, in all its details, for us an unmapped riddle of which eye and mind have no clear conception.

I have often been asked, "What were the difficulties of the campaign?"—for the uninitiated have sensed that there were difficulties—and I have answered, "Our greatest enemy to overcome was the ever-blinding, ever-foiling bush and jungle growth; our second enemy was the intensely hot climate, and subsequent disease; the third enemy was the shortage of adequate rations; and the fourth enemy was the grim tenacity of a stubborn and worthy foe." There you have the four essential conditions that made the East African Campaign a long one. But, undoubtedly, the main condition, the one that can never be overlooked, is that, in a territory 176,210 square miles larger than Germany—which is seven-eighths larger than the whole area of the German Empire—the country was a vast, unbounded wilderness of bush, with ready cover to conceal all the armies of the world. Into that blank area were placed our tiny pawns of armies, to move and counter-move, with the touch of blind men, in pursuit of peoples who were, in their knowledge of the country, like wild animals in their native haunts.

And there for a time we must leave this subject, and the enemy—free like-wild animals in the bush—while I return to our camp life at Tulo.

On the 19th of September, leaving Nkessa's, I rejoined my unit at Tulo, and remained there ten days, while the operations of our column stood more or less at a standstill. Apparently our chase from Morogoro had entailed even greater difficulties than usual to our line of communication, and a breathing space had become imperative to attend to road repairs in the hills behind, and to augment our failing supplies.

Ultimately it transpired that our onward-pressing advance had come to a prolonged halt that was to confine us to this unhealthy area for three and a half wearisome months, while rains fell incessantly in the Ulugúru hills in the rear and blocked the road to almost all traffic. Hence we were constrained to wait in patience, holding on to our front in this low country, and subsisting on such rations as could be got through to us, while here too it rained, though in lesser quantity than in the hills. When we came down out of the hills into the low country our battalion camped for nineteen days at Tulo, before moving on, on the 30th of September, to take over permanent positions at Old and New Kissaki on the Mgeta River.

A, few records of Tulo may be interesting, and I will endeavour to follow our existence there for a few days.

Tulo, 21st Sept., 1916—Heavy rains overnight and all to-day, causing much discomfort, since we have no shelter or clothing against such weather. We have been camping under mere sun-shelters, hastily erected, and protection only from the heat. We had been caught unprepared, and as penalty slept the night in soaking blankets on the sodden ground, while today has passed without chance to dry anything, not even our wet blankets. To-morrow, the ambulance will attend more fever cases than ordinarily.

Tulo, 22nd Sept—Rain has ceased, and everyone in camp is today employed rectifying their shelters against a recurrence of downpour by rigging, over their camp spaces, steep-pitched roofs, framed with green poles cut from the bush, and thatched with compact layers of long grass gathered from the surrounding country by our porters. In the afternoon I rode out south-west across the river to look for game, and secured three reed-buck in open, dried-out swamp country.

Tulo, 23rd Sept—Remained in camp all day. Overnight heavy firing was heard in the direction of Nkessa's village. Today a crocodile was shot in the Mwuha River: it measured 13 feet 1 inch.

Tulo, 25th Sept—Nothing new today. No fresh news of *our*

war, or of the European war, of which we get but scraps of information at intervals. Spent the morning on battery drills and on machine-gun instruction. In this country, where sickness is so rife, it is impossible to keep an efficient gun team together for any length of time. Old hands slip away each week, and men to replace them have endlessly to be instructed in the intricate mechanism of the gun whenever halt gives opportunity. In the afternoon out for a hunt, to keep fit, and to look for buck meat, chiefly for porter food, as their ration issue is very short. But today I searched without success, principally through having a local native with me who purposely, or foolishly, took me over what proved to be very poor game country. Nearing camp on the way home, I shot four of those delicious table birds—the wild guinea-fowl, which I have— wanting a shot gun—taken to shooting with our ·303 service rifle; which indeed now serves for the killing of anything from a partridge upwards.

Next day, still wanting meat, I rode out on horseback and, with the assistance of my porter followers, brought in the meat of four reed-buck. On the 28th of September I again went out with the same purpose, and secured three water-buck, animals about the size of a mule and of the same dark mouse colour. In this way were the natives tided over some bad ration days.

Before passing on, I must mention a strange incident that occurred last night. A great pack of hyenas, like a pack of timber wolves, came from the bush to the east, right through the centre of the camp, snarling and howling and fighting at our very hut doors as they passed, arousing the whole camp to wakefulness and astonishment with their gruesome, fiendish uproar. The camp, in pitch darkness, was a regular wolf garden for some minutes, ere the last of the howling, quarrelling mob had gone through, and passed beyond the camp. Why such a thing occurred no one could tell next morning; the impression given was that the whole band was chasing something, a wounded buck perhaps, or one or two outcasts of their own kind; but, in any case, they were so intent on their business that they knew no fear of our presence, for they went through our camp, in their wild excitement, just as if they were going down a main city street, though in ordinary temperament such surroundings would have filled them with the greatest suspicion and fear.

So much for the small events of bush life while we lay at Tulo.

After the usual reorganising, preparatory to abandon a camp we had been settled in for some days, we left Tulo in the early morning of 30th September, and trekked forward to Nkessa's, *en route* for Kissaki; there to take over the positions captured some time ago by South African forces, in conjunction with operations on this side.

Meantime we had learned that we were to remain on in the country, a reduced but a hard-dying Imperial unit, though in the latter months of this year a great many exhausted white troops were sent back to better climes—I believe, in all, some 12,000, the larger number of whom, excepting a battalion of the Loyal North Lancs., and the 2nd Rhodesians, had landed in the country in the early part of the year. These troops were replaced, in time, by newly raised battalions of King's African Rifles, and by the Nigerian Brigade—all of them native regiments, accustomed to the hot African climate.

The advance to the Rufiji had by this time been definitely postponed, and our command was now concerned in holding the Mgeta River front at all vital points, and in patrolling, continuously and alertly, the intervening country from post to post. Our battalion was ordered to Kissaki Fort, and to Camp A— the old Arab fort of Kissaki, and about two miles south of the present fort. In taking up these positions we were on the extreme right of the Mgeta front, a front that lay virtually east and west along the course of the river. Our camp at

124

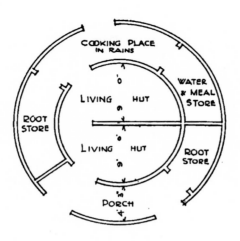

COOKING PLACE
IN RAINS

LIVING   HUT

WATER
& MEAL
STORE

ROOT
STORE

LIVING   HUT

ROOT
STORE

PORCH

NATIVE KRAAL.

Old Kissaki was within a square compound, walled in by an ancient hedge of impenetrable, needle-leaved cactus. Within the compound were some old stone foundations of long-demolished buildings, and in the centre an old unused stone-built well. Outside the compound a road ran in from the east to the very entrance of the square, to turn off abruptly there and head north on the way to New Kissaki Fort. The road outside the compound, in both directions, was bordered with solid-looking avenues of large, thick-leaved mango trees, while underneath those trees, on the road from the east, nestled the shaded grass huts of a score or two of peaceful natives. In the neighbourhood of the fort some land was cultivated, but where not, it grew dense and rank, with tall grass and low bush. In the big rains of February—April the entire country adjacent to the river is two or three feet under water, say the natives; and they tell of how they then go to live in the hills. This locality had a considerable native population, and their huts and mealie patches are to be found at intervals near to the banks of the river along its course.

These native habitations have with them a certain human homeliness, a certain attractiveness, that is altogether foreign. Picture a group of tall, full-bodied trees with thick foliage, dark and green, from which issues the pensive, melodious *"co-coo-oo"* of African doves toward the eve of a throbbing, sunscorched day, when the air is cooling, and you are fortunate to have leisure to notice that the scenes and the sounds are pleasant and restful. These are the mango tree (*mwembe*)—trees of blessed shade against the hot sun, and trees that, when the leaves are ready to fall, in October or November, give a rich harvest of delicious mango fruit.

It is here, close to their sheltering shade, that the native huts are grouped; huts with a great proportion of steep roof of weather-darkened grass, and with low squat walls of baked reddish mud. Here naked children play around the tree-trunk roots, in the shade, while old shrivelled-up women, or labouring wives, together under the hut-eaves, croon their soft Swahili folk-songs, in tune with the doves in the trees, in tune, indeed, with all that is African. About the habitations are some patches of cultivation—a not extensive irregular area of ground cleared, without choice of fair angles or straight lines, in any old haphazard way, wherever the bush could most easily be cleared, or where the soil held most richness and moisture. Here and there in the clearing stands a great wintry looking, sparsely leaved wild fig tree (*mcuyu*), a landmark to the eyes of all. On those clearings are grown millet (*mtama*) and maize (*mahindi*), which is the harvest of the native——his bread, as it were, his chief staple food. Part of the crop is standing, twice the height of man, tall, clustering reed-canes with long ribbon leaves and bending, burdened seed-heads, caught into motion, and rustling in the light, undulating wind. Here, moreover, from the neighbouring bush, numerous doves fly, swift-winged and grey, to feed on the ground among the stems; to search out the broken heads that have fallen, or to perch, with some effort to balance, on swinging plant top to plunder the ripened head. Part of the crop has been cut as need required, and, in the open, the stem-strewn stubble lies, straw brown, and level, and tinder dry.

Such is the common aspect of the native habitations in this neighbourhood.

Within the compound we built our huts of shelter—for owing to transport difficulties we never had tents—and strongly entrenched the perimeter against attack. Water we carry from the river, which is about half a mile south down a dusty track between bushes; and since this same water is essential to existence here, vigilant pickets guard the river drift, day and night.

Here at Camp A, as the old fort was designated, we had a period of heavy duties, busily fortifying the position, while rations became shorter and shorter.

On 3rd October I record:

Another day of fatigues. Every one more overstrained than usual, for we are now in low country that is excessively hot and relaxing. It is difficult to keep up good spirits all round. Unfortunately there is no ration improvement, and no word of fresh kit coming, of which all are much in need. Notice shirtless men in camp, with badly sun-burned backs, and men on the march without socks. One sees, in the brave suffering of men, many things in these days to make one's heart sore and sad. Today General Sheppard, the man who has won the popularity of our men, and of all, visiting the camp from Dakawa, paraded the remnant of our force and spoke encouragingly of the ration shortage, thanking all for enduring the hardships so cheerfully, and promising at least some improvement in four days' time.

At this time, too, most men are without even the solace of tobacco, having run completely out of it, though some tackle the crude native stuff, and make of it cigarettes by rolling it in paper or in dry mealie-cob sheaths. At best this was a hot, rank smoke which some could put up with, but which many had to forgo, after a brave trial or two.

But light may glint through even the worst of shadows, and a day or two later some parcels reached camp from home, and priceless were they to their lucky recipients. I wish those at home who had sent those gifts could have witnessed, even though it might have brought tears to their eyes, those ragged men rejoicing over the gifts that meant so much to them in their need, and were not to be bought for their weight in gold. Yet, after all, they were but little things; such as a pair of socks, some packets of Gold Flake cigarettes, a cake of soap, a candle or two, and a few tins of sardines or biscuits. Nothing at all when you are living in civilisation or near to it, but everything to men heart-hungry and half-starved of any luxury for nigh on two years.

Yes! We had our *mean* days in Africa, plenty of them. We had had them before, we were having them here, and we are certain to experience them again, but in all our roughing it those dark days at Kissaki cannot be surpassed, and they were the days that found our spirits at the lowest ebb.

During our stay in the Kissaki area, I will ramble over some of the incidents of daily life as they chanced to come along. If they should appear more personal than ought to be, in my endeavour to be accurate, through describing incidents that were known directly to me, I would like you to forget the *I* and imagine any one of us in that character, for, besides the regular routine of patrols, all were employed on a variety of similar duties, arduous and otherwise, and found our little pleasures, one in the manner of the other, when the opportunity chanced our way.

Kissaki, 5th Oct—Carrying out orders received, to make sketch survey of Mgeta River and neighbourhood east of drift. Found the river-banks of tall grass in many places impenetrable, and therefore, to secure the principal bearings and distances, I, and the two men who were with me, took to the water and waded, waist-deep, some two miles down the centre of the broad stream. It was, since the water was warm, not such an unpleasant proceeding as it would appear, so long as no enemy, or crocodiles, put in an appearance; and neither were seen. On the spits of sand on the river-side, where they occasionally appeared, were many fresh footprints of elephant and hippopotamus, telling that they habit this district in numbers, and haunt the river at night and at daybreak. Today fifteen German Askaris passed wide of our picket at the river drift. In the evening, cavalry reported a company of the enemy camped close to the drift, and additional precautions were taken in camp against an attack. But the night passed quietly, and no attempt was made by the enemy, to seize and hold the river-bank, as was thought they might do. Our forces here are small—growing smaller daily through sickness—and a strong attack of the enemy might now make our position difficult to hold.

Kissaki, 8th Oct—This afternoon one of my porters rushed excitedly into camp and breathlessly told that three Germans were cutting the telegraph wires on the road north of the camp. Not, on the spur of the moment, being able to find the O.C., I went unauthorised in chase with two machine-gun volunteers, after I had left word that I had gone to keep in touch with the enemy, and asking that reinforcements follow on later. I found that the enemy had been alarmed by our porters, who were in numbers in the bush, cutting wood, and had got a start of us, but we went in pursuit nevertheless, and after a hot chase of about three miles we came in sight of the enemy. We had crossed the river away back, and had followed out the chase over native tracks, and were now far over our front. In passing a group of native *kraals* we learned that the enemy, who had just passed through ahead of us, were eleven strong, so when we sighted them, on the other side of a bare mealie-field, we paused, awaiting developments. And while we thus lay watching under cover of some bush, up came seven Indian cavalry, who had been sent out from camp. Immediately they charged on the enemy, whom we pointed out to them, outpacing us altogether down the side of the field, though we followed at a run. I thought then that we had the raiders sure—but we were doomed to disappointment. The enemy, before the cavalry reached them, scattered in the bush, to the left or to the right?—the cavalry, nor we, could tell not where—and escaped under the rank jungle cover. Reluctantly, and after much unsuccessful searching of likely groups of bush, we gave up at dusk and returned to camp, feeling that our little adventure had deserved a more fitting finish. However, I think we thoroughly frightened the enemy, for the wires were not again interfered with while we lay at Kissaki.

Kissaki, 15th Oct—Seven German Askaris gave themselves up overnight. They report food scarce, and also that numbers of natives are deserting and going off west through the bush, their purpose to try to find their way back to their homes. They also say, as we have heard before, that the German carriers are partially bound when in camp, so that they cannot run away in the night, if they wanted to escape.

Then I find a few entries when all was not as it should be and a little cry of impatience had crept in:

Kissaki, 10th Oct—Bad night; suffering from dysentery. Weak and lay on my grass-bed all day.

11th Oct—Little better today and trying to get around duties. Feeling about *all in* now, but must stick it out with the others, and trust that the sickness will pass off.

19th Oct—Feeling better today and cheerier, but I wish, since I've lost patience, that we could get along with *the Show*, and then be quit of Africa for a time, for I have a passionate desire that we should be free to change, just for a little, the colour and the quality of a long-familiar picture whose strange characteristics are now indelible. Sometimes, I'm afraid, I feel as if I was in prison, and long for the freedom of the life beyond these prison walls. Those are times when thoughts quickly fly in and out the old scenes—dear old familiar scenes—and they are touched now with a deep and a sure appreciation. Would that they could stay; would that, by the strength of their willingness, they could lift me in body over the vast space and set me in some fair, peaceful land! But, alas! So quickly as I write they are back again, exhausted, and fluttering in the hated African sun-glare. Nevertheless, for the hour, I am restless as those thoughts. This campaign, this adventure of war, has been a long game of patience, and I feel mad, poor wight, at times to chuck away the cards and run. But, after all, I know that all is as it should be, and that the hand must be strong to win. Yet it would be a very beautiful day in my eyes were it ever to come to pass, this pictured freedom from war and bloodshed, though for the present it is so far down the long blind trail of the uncertain road before me that I may but carry the memory of things that have been, and of things that are ideal.

So may I ponder—so may others here, though they are but thoughts that well up for a moment, and then fade away into the far distance of space, where, like the setting sun, or the mists on the hills, they may mingle with the mysteries of beyond. However, I have paused long enough with such thoughts, and will leave them now, perhaps a little reverently, and go on with the record of other days for neither thought nor the span of a day can hold steadfast for long, without the intervention of onward passing time, and change to other scenes.

Kissaki, 3rd Nov—I am back in camp again, after being away seven days on reconnaissance up into the Ulugúru mountains, to try to find a suitable track, back over the hills to Matombo, for porter transport during the approaching rains, when the low road, via Tulo, will be flooded. My party was made up of privates Taylor and Wilson, six native carriers, and a shrewd old native who was supposed to know the country, and, contrary to usual experience, did know it. We found the outermost point of our journey at Kasanga, overlooking Matombo, and high up in the mountains—elevation, 3,900 feet—amongst majestic hill-slopes and fair deep valleys which were cultivated by the numerous inhabitants of the hills, who dwelt everywhere, in their little bits of *crofts*, like the ancient highlander of mediaeval ages. We were two days out from camp when we found ourselves in this land of plenty, and land of great beauty; for the scenery surpassed anything we had previously seen in Africa. Up in the mountain heights the air was cool, almost cold; mists fitfully swept over the peaks and dropped like waterfalls into the valleys; it rained, then cleared again—all ever-changing the picture, and the lights and shades on the mountain slopes, and in the valleys—truly it was a most enchanting country. The trail outward, up hill and down valley, and along the line of least resistance, proved to be thirty-one miles in distance, all of which was measured by counting the paces as we trudged along, and surveyed by many compass bearings. From such data I was able completely to map the route, on my return to camp, and this was the manner in which I carried out all such work, when detailed information was wanted.

On the return journey, after descending from the highest ranges, and when drawing away from the last of the cultivated area, the party encountered a small herd of elephant feeding amongst bamboos, and loudly breaking their way along a wide valley bottom. Taylor and I, both armed with ·303 rifles, cut off the track and went to try to get a shot at the beasts—both very keen to bag an elephant. Successfully we worked up-wind on them, and finally drew near to two animals partly hidden in the fringe of the bamboo belt. I doubted the killing capacity of our rifles, but, when we fired, it transpired that both animals dropped—though in the thick cover, for the moment, we couldn't be sure of the full effect of our shots—one dead, and the other emitting the most dreadful trumpet blasts, that echoed and re-echoed, like thunder, in the enclosed valley. The wounded animal could, apparently, not run away, but we dared not, meantime, go any nearer to him, in case he should charge us down in the tall, tangled grass, where, for us, running was well-nigh impossible. Therefore we decided to leave him for a time, and return to where we had left Wilson and the porters. We found our porter loads scattered broadcast on the track, but not a black was to be seen, for, at the trumpeting of the wounded elephant, they had scattered and fled in mortal terror. Wilson, who was armed with a revolver only, and could not take part in the shooting, in the midst of the uproar had been, while standing on the track, almost knocked down by the rush past of a startled water-buck. We shouted for the porters, and, one by one, they appeared, reluctantly, from various directions, to be chaffed and laughed at. They were all wildly excited when we said we had one or two elephants shot, and lying in the bamboos below. Taylor and I had both been suffering from malaria throughout the day—brought out by the cold in the hills—so we decided on a drink of tea to refresh us, and hurried the boys about it, while excited talk ran high. Twenty minutes later, though we could still hear an occasional movement in the bamboos, we decided to venture down to our quarry, but nothing on earth would tempt any of the blacks to come. Soon I saw our quarry, badly wounded, but still able to move about a bit. A moment later I put the elephant down like a log, with a fatal bullet, and we could hear him venting great sobbing breaths as life gave out. We now ventured close up, and saw him lying on his side with all legs out. Now and again his huge head raised, but only to relax to the ground again. By and by he was quite still, and then we went up to him. We were looking at him, highly delighted, since it was our first elephant, when Wilson cried "Look out!" pointing, as he did so, to our right. We wheeled round to see, indistinctly through the canes and grass, the head and the great forward-thrust ears of an elephant quite close to us—I fired, and again rang out that appalling trumpet cry. Soon, as all was quiet, we went forward cautiously, to exclaim our surprise when we found a great cow elephant dead—killed by one of our first shots—and a young bull fatally wounded beside her. The wounded animal was dispatched, and, after some trouble, and assurances that there was not another elephant alive in Africa, we persuaded the black boys to venture down, and to start cutting out the tusks from the skull base with their long-bladed, heavy, wood-chopping knives. I left them, then, to get under the shade of a tree, and to roll myself in my blanket, for by this time I was absolutely exhausted, and in high fever. Water had been found near-by, and I had given orders that we would camp here till the morning. I hazily remember looking out of my blanket about 5 p.m., when the sun was lowering, to see the tusk trophies lying close to me

134

and the native boys, "happy as kings," smoking huge pieces of elephant trunk, placed on bamboo racks over well-fed fires.

Next day, in the morning before we moved on, troops of natives began to arrive from the hills to cut up, and smoke, and part roast, the elephant meat—to carry it off, when ready, to their homes. It was good to see their simple rejoicing at securing such plentiful food.

On one other occasion I ran across elephants when on reconnaissance work. This was about six miles south-west of Kissaki, at hot springs at the northern end of Magi-ya-Weta Hill. I had been out looking over the country, with the view to finding a road route, when I found that large herds of elephant had been recently at the water below the springs, and in some places had wrecked the bush-forest when feeding—for an elephant, if wanting to reach the upper growth, thinks nothing of grasping a tree-trunk, and pulling downwards with his mighty weight (a large elephant weighs about seven tons) until the tree, which has commonly a diameter of six to eight inches, snaps off like a broken match, a yard or two above the ground.

On my return to camp from reconnaissance I happily received permission to go out again in quest of the elephants; and set out next day with my fellow-officer, Martin Ryan—a Rhodesian, who was an experienced elephant hunter.

Kissaki, 5th Dec—Left camp at 6 a.m., Captain Ryan, self, and nine natives. We camped about a mile from the springs at 12 noon. On viewing the ground, which was new to Ryan, we decided to make the noon camp our base, and here left six of the boys when we started out again at 3 p.m. About 4.30 p.m., when still searching for the large fresh track of bull elephant, we had the extraordinary luck to see three large elephants, with fine tusks, coming along the edge of a belt of forest, on our right flank and towards us. Ryan, beckoning to me, immediately set out after them—after he had dropped a handful of dust to test the wind—and, crouching and running, we were soon very close to them, while the short-sighted brutes, intent on feeding as they moved along in single file, were still unaware of our presence. When at not more than fifteen yards from our quarry, Ryan dropped on his knees, and fired on the elephant opposite him (the centre one of the three), trying to get in the brain shot, just in front of the ear. On the report of Ryan's shot the rear elephant cleared off the way it had come, while the leading elephant swung wide and then crossed back, at full run, attempting to rejoin its companion. This elephant I now gave my attention to—for I had hesitated, while the huge bulk of Ryan's elephant interrupted my view—and got in four shots which apparently had no effect, though I felt fairly certain that the second and fourth shots had been true. I followed the brute at a run, but, for the moment, couldn't find trace of him where he had disappeared in thicker forest. Meantime Ryan's elephant had recovered, and had got away with six shots in him, delivered at hand-to-hand range; so I rejoined my comrade, to find him empty-handed and fearing he had *mulled* his chance. However, we now set about tracking his elephant over ground very difficult to follow tracks on, as it was hard and dry, and strewn with dead leaves, and had been trampled over recently by numerous elephants. Again and again we went off on a false track, until Ryan, whose keen eye was looking for such minute signs as a single freshly crushed leaf, or a small broken twig, stem, or grass, would declare he was at a loss once more. At last, nearing dusk, Ryan said, "We'll have one more try and then go to camp,"—and the "one more try" found our prey, outstretched and dead, under the trees of a thick growth of forest. He was a great brute with a splendid pair of tusks, the largest Ryan had ever secured, and this was his fifty-seventh elephant. A few measurements I took next day were:

A Good Bag : 268½ lb. of Ivory.

	FT	INS
LENGTH—FROM SNOUT OF TRUNK TO ROOT OF TAIL	19	3
LENGTH OF TRUNK	6	6
HEIGHT TO SHOULDER	10	6
GIRTH OF BODY	18	0
LENGTH OF TUSKS	6	1½

WEIGHT OF TUSKS, 58 IB. AND 59½ IB. = 117½ IB

We returned to camp highly delighted with our success, and reached it with difficulty in the dark. On the way to camp we encountered a cow elephant feeding in a swamp, and Ryan took considerable pains to pass it, at some distance, without being detected, for he was afraid that if it had a calf and scented danger, it would charge, and prove a furious, fearless brute. I, in my ignorance, would, perhaps, not have foreseen danger there, but it afterwards made me think a bit of the risk of elephant-hunting, when I saw this seasoned hunter treating a single animal with such great respect and care. But Ryan told me that you may only have to make a mistake once, and pay the full penalty of it with your life. He said there are few men, who have hunted elephants long, who are not in the end caught; and long is his list of those who have been killed in Rhodesia by an enraged elephant, at the far end of their hunting days.

We could hear many elephants moving near camp during the night—a herd of cow elephants, Ryan conjectured, for at this season the bulls roam singly or in very small numbers.

At daybreak next morning we set out for the scene of yesterday's adventure, taking all the boys with us. On reaching our quarry we started the natives to break in the skull to the root of each tusk, an undertaking that, even with axes that we had brought for the purpose, kept the boys incessantly labouring for nigh on two hours, so hard and so great are the bones of an elephant's head. Meantime, I and a native had gone off to try to track my elephant, starting from the point of shooting and working out to where I'd last seen him. Soon, following his track step by step, we found he had swung to the right, and I then knew I had overrun him yesterday. In a quarter of an hour more, great was my joy to come on him stone dead, not 500 yards from where Ryan's elephant lay. Again he proved to be all that he had looked (for Ryan had yesterday declared the leading elephant to be the best one), a grand old bull, with a beautiful pair of tusks, weighing, it later proved, 74 lb. and 77½ lb., = 151½ lb., and measuring 6 ft. 5½ in. in length. He was shot through the lungs, and his right hind-leg was crumpled up under him, so probably he was hit somewhere there also, though it was, of course, impossible to move him and see.

We got back to camp in the late afternoon with our loads of ivory, which took six men to carry, and next day trekked to Kissaki, where our arrival with such fine trophies caused much interest and not a little excitement.

The last weeks of the year 1916 marked various activities on our front, in preparation for another advance. Trees were felled in large numbers in the river neighbourhood, and with such crude timber more than one stout bridge was thrown across the Mgeta River, opposite our camps.

Away, even to Kirengwe, ten miles west of the old *boma*, a party of us went out to cut a twelve-foot road through an otherwise impenetrable forest belt, in preparation for a wide flank advance. In those last weeks of the year, also, some of us did considerable reconnaissance work, and were interested in gaining as much knowledge as possible of the enemy's country across the river, particularly in the direction of Wiransi Hill, which was on the enemy's line of retreat from Dakawa.

Supplies, too, had improved; and our forces were strengthened and augmented by other units. Captain Selous, who had been invalided home to England some months before, arrived in camp on the 16th of December with a draft of 150 fresh men; and at a time when our effective strength was very much reduced through sickness and exhaustion.

Selous looked hale and hearty, and the grand old man he was. How fine an example of loyalty he gave, in thus, at his great age, returning again to the front to fight his country's battles! It was pleasant to see him back amongst us again, for his own sake, and for the additional joy of hearing directly of the old country, and of how we were faring in the great war at home. Of course talk drifted to hunting, and we had to exchange news since last we met: he of a large butterfly collection which he had collected in the first year and had taken home, and we of our hunting since he left. Meantime machine-gun porters were building the *Bwana M'Kubwa* (the Big Master) a grass *banda*, and soon Selous was comfortably sheltered among us. I mention this because it was here, at the old Kissaki *boma*, that Selous was destined to have his last brief rest from travel, his last sleep in comfort, ere he met his death on the field of battle some two weeks later.

On the 20th of December it was known that a move was anticipated, and preparations for trekking were commenced. It was decided, in due course, that we advance on the 27th, but on that date, and on the day previous, heavy rains fell and the move was postponed, while at the same time it was reported that, owing to the storm, our heavy guns were stuck on the road beyond Tulo. If rains continued it would be most unfortunate. Undoubtedly the wet season was near, and, I remember, Selous had grave doubts of the weather at this period, and feared that the whole operation might be stopped, for he knew the swift change the big rains would bring about, and how flooded and impassable the country would become. However, after five days of rain, the weather cleared somewhat, and we had orders on New Year's Eve that to-morrow the Mgeta position would be attacked.

Meantime, on the 30th, a column, under General Beves, moved through our camp, *en route* to Kissaki Fort and thence to Kirengwe, to advance, away on the right flank, on Mkalinso on the Rufiji River.

The early morning of New Year's Day found our forces across the river at points along a wide twenty-mile front, and attacking the enemy's elaborate entrenchments wherever they were known to exist.

Under the direction of General Sheppard, the fighting on our column took place opposite Dakawa. Part of the force made a frontal attack on the enemy's first-line trenches, and the remainder, after crossing the river by the new bridge south of our camp, advanced from a westerly direction, and successfully intercepted the enemy in their retirement from their first line on to their second line. Here hand-to-hand fighting ensued, and the foiled enemy Askaris three times charged with fixed bayonets in their attempts to break through in ordered formation, but in all they were defeated and scattered in the bush, in the end to escape in disorder.

The 130th Baluchis did splendidly in this fighting and bore the brunt of the attack. Losses on both sides were severe, as a result of the closeness and the fierceness of the fighting. Toward noon the fighting on our front had eased off, and, with the enemy scattered and in full retreat in the bush, we continued southward on the Behobeho road, camping at 11.30 p.m., when the column had advanced some fifteen miles, and was in touch with our force in occupation of Wiransi: for a small detachment, travelling through the bush the previous night, had surprised and captured Wiransi early in the day, taking some white prisoners and some stores.

During the day operations to our east had been progressing with equal success. On the centre General Cunliffe, with the Nigerians, had advanced from Nkessa's out to Kiderengwe, clearing the enemy from the strong entrenchments before him on the south bank of the Mgeta River.

On the left flank, a column under General Lyall made a hard cross-country trek in crossing westerly from Kiruru to cut the Dunthumi— Kiderengwe road, on reaching which they intercepted enemy retiring from before the central force.

Among other incidents during the fighting, a company from this column charged and captured one of the renowned 4·1 Koenigsberg guns.

Thus evening found the whole network of entrenchments on the Mgeta River front—so long the halting-place of operations—completely in our hands, and the enemy in full retreat.

The night of 1st January passed uneventfully. Bugle-less, drum-less *réveillé*—silent as always in enemy country—was at 4.30 a.m. and we trekked soon afterwards, but only into Wiransi, where we halted until 4 o'clock in the evening; then continuing, we advanced out on the Behobeho track some three to four miles, before striking off south-westerly through tall grass and fairly open bush in the direction of the Fuga hills. Aided by the light of a full moon, the column kept on until midnight, when the hitherto level bush became more uneven, and thick bush belts were encountered among low hills and *dongas* of rough gravel surface. Halt was called in a fairly clear space of tall grass, but almost immediately exclamations of pain and acute irritation were heard on all sides from much-provoked individuals, and the air was literally full of abuse—we had camped among a swarm of fighting ants, who straightway attacked the bare legs and arms and faces of everyone, in no half-hearted manner, but with all the malice of their angered millions. It was suggested that we move to another camping-ground at once, but no order came to that effect, and by and by, when the attacks abated, we dropped off to sleep, one by one, too tired to continue to kill the more vengeful of the ants that still bit deep into quivering weather-toughened skins.

Next day we continued on, but made progress slowly in the neighbourhood of Mount Fuga, hampered by river-beds and their precipitous descents and ascents. We put in a trying day's trek, considerably exhausted by the heat and oppressive atmosphere of the enclosed bush, and finally made camp at dusk between Mount Fuga and Behobeho—which was known to be occupied by the enemy.

In conjunction with our force a column to the east are advancing on the Behobeho track, and we heard that column in action today. We, on our part, now outflank the enemy from the west.

On 4th January we moved before daylight, and slowly headed in toward Behobeho. An hour or two later we made a prolonged halt, and lay hidden under cover of the bush in widely extended formation, while north-east we could hear the other column in heavy action. Anxiously we waited—impatiently—but no enemy fell into the ambush. After a time scouts, who had been watching the track which was but a short distance ahead, hurriedly reported that enemy in scattered forces were retiring along it. We then moved forward on the track-road, to take up positions closely viewing it. As we drew near to the road some enemy were seen approaching. On these we immediately opened machine-gun and rifle fire, surprising them completely, and inflicting severe casualties. Notwithstanding this they retaliated, gamely enough for a little, but our firing wore them down, and soon those that remained were silent, and fleeing in the bush. We were now astride the road in the rear of enemy forces, but to the wily foe, aided by the nature of the country, this only meant the brief blocking of their line of retreat. They would, and did, avoid the danger in their path by taking to the wide area of vacant bush to the east of the track, and scattered there to meet at some prearranged rendezvous, in a distant zone of safety.

Meantime, having cut on to the track very close to the village of Behobeho—which we later learned harboured a large German camp—a lively action soon developed with forces entrenched before the village. Directly north of the level ground on which Behobeho is situated, there are some low, gravel-covered ridges, facing the village, and those we advanced on to, and there a line was established, while fierce fighting continued for some hours, with our men lying on the almost red-hot ground of the ridge crests, beneath a scorching, merciless sun. Men who had been exposed to African sun for nigh on two years, and were skin-hardened and browned to the colour of leather, nevertheless suffered serious sunburn, and were blistered and peeled like delicately skinned children, on the following day, so great had been the heat reflected from the white gravel crystals on which they had lain. It was a trying fight in other uncommon ways, for, though we were in fair positions against the enemy before the village, we were fully exposed to sniping from the tall trees which shaded the village, and we suffered a considerable part of our casualties on that account. It was here that Captain Selous was killed, when commanding his company in attack. His death caused a deep-felt whisper of gravity and regret to pass along the line of faithful soldiers, who loved him in uncommon manner, as their officer and as their grand old fearless man. Here occurred an incident which speaks volumes for Selous's understanding of natives—on the just consideration of whom he held strong opinions, and a broad generous view of kindliness toward untutored humanity in any form, tempered with the latent authority of a strong man. When Selous was killed, his native servant, Ramazani—who had been a gun-bearer of Selous's before he war—was overcome with grief and swore to avenge his master's death, and through the remainder of the engagement he exposed himself in absolute fearlessness in his grim rage against the foe. At the end of the day he claimed with conviction that he had killed the man who had killed his master. About 4 p.m. Behobeho was occupied, and the enemy in full retreat to Rufiji, which was now but another day's march farther on. Later in the evening the eastern column, which had had severe fighting in dislodging the enemy from entrenched positions on the road farther back, joined our force here. At Behobeho Captain Selous and a few of the faithful *lean brown men* were buried in the shade of a great baobab tree. Thus the famous hunter finished a career that had been full of great risks and great adventures, fighting for his country, at the age of sixty-five years—seeing through his last undertaking in Africa as, perhaps, he would have chosen it should be, for this was the continent he had explored the outer frontiers of, more than any other living man, and in the early days, when Africa was *darkest* Africa, and primitive races and strange diseases far more difficult to contend with than they are today. Here he had found his life's work, and had risen to renown; and here, on the soil of Africa, he was destined to die.

The next four days, being wounded, I remained behind, and missed our occupation of the north bank of the great Rufiji River. But bandaged, and fit but for a crippled left *wing*, I was able to rejoin my battalion at Kibambawe, and again take on my machine-gun command, which was otherwise without an officer, since few remained fit at this stage. I found all our forces on the banks of the Rufiji, and dug in against the enemy away across the marsh-banked stream which, from memory, had a width of from 700 to 1,000 yards.

The opposite bank had been subjected to searching machine-gun fire during the first two days, and now the enemy were quiet, and to effect a crossing of our forces we—and also the western column, which had reached Mkalinso—were apparently but waiting the construction of rafts, and the arrival of the row-boats which were being brought up, all this distance inland, from Dar-es-Salaam to surmount the difficulty of bridging this river. However, our battalion remained but three more mildly eventful days on the Rufiji front: then, being relieved, we had to commence a long fourteen days' march back to Morogoro, there to enter rest-camp, and ultimately, some time later, to be sent from Dar-es-Salaam. to South Africa to recuperate for three months at *the Cape*.

The big rains were approaching. It transpired that they broke on 25th January, soon after our forces had crossed and effected a lodgement on the south shores of the Rufiji— and there active operations ended for some months, while the country was deluged with torrential tropical rains.

A dispatch of General Hoskins, then commanding the East Africa Forces—since General Smuts had a few weeks previously been called to the War Cabinet in London—stated:

> By the 27th January the lines of communication from Mikessa (on the Central Railway) to Kibambawe were interrupted by the washing away of bridges and the flooding of roads, and operations in all areas were henceforth seriously hampered by the untimely rains.
>
> In the Mgeta and Rufiji valleys roads constructed with much skill and labour, over which motor transport ran continually in January, were traversed with difficulty and much hardship a month later by porters wading for miles in water above their waists.

To native regiments was left the unpleasant task of *holding on* under those dreadfully trying conditions, and there they remained, through the months to come, marooned on their little bits of dry islands, with flood water ankle deep around them; while we, lucky people, were out of it for the time being, and were at last to enjoy rest and change, and to witness, in South Africa, the civilisation and society to which our long-bushed eyes and minds had been completely estranged for nigh on two years.

CHAPTER 7

The End of the Campaign
on German Soil

Our glorious rest of three months at the Cape came to an end—months which had been filled with the joy and appreciation of men who had come out of scenes that had borne something of nightmare into the full light of life, among people of their own kind, in a beautiful, peaceful land. The intellectual uplifting was supreme. Minds that were fever-weakened, and depressed, and unresponsive—and few had not been affected by prolonged hardship and equatorial climate—came again to life and ordinary buoyant activity.

But our rest was over. On 12th May, 1917, we regretfully bade good-bye to Cape Town and travelled by train overland through the bleak Karroo Veldt, and on to Durban, to embark again there for East Africa on 19th May. Durban had for some days been the gathering-point for this movement, and many troops were congregated here when we arrived. Five ships, loaded with troops and stores, made up the convoy which sailed from Durban for East Africa, a considerable reinforcement that promised an immediate recommencement of offensive operations now that the rainy season was over. Then, too, on the *Caronia,* which was one of the ships of the convoy, were General Van Deventer and General Beves, and their staffs, hastening back to take again the field. This great liner, the *Caronia,* was on her way to India with troops, and was only to touch in on the East African coast, but serious combustion set in in her coal bunkers and threatened to delay her voyage, and therefore, on nearing our destination, those of us going to East Africa transferred to naval craft at sea, and thenceforward proceeded to port.

On the morning of 29th May, I and a few comrades, who had been travelling overnight on an auxiliary cruiser, found ourselves on deck, and the ship standing off the low white sand shore of Lindi Bay, a mile or more from land. Thus we had again come in sight of East Africa—again we looked on the silent land that lay before us, darkened with that unforgettable growth of bush thicket that reached to the very borders of the sea. We viewed the shore with mixed feelings: adventure still held an attraction to us, but the country had, in its latent possibilities, the power to appal the searchings of imagination, and it was with feelings more sober than otherwise that we contemplated the land before us. For there lay the bush-land, as it had always lain before us, an over-dark picture which no man could surely read, though he knew, since he had seen it in another light, and had looked at it closely, that behind the foreground in view there was concealed the vague lines of startling drama.

Meantime a small steam tug had put out of Lindi, and when this drew alongside we boarded her, and, bidding cheery good-bye to the officers of the cruiser, who had been brief but the best of comrades, the little tug *jug-jugged* earnestly in for shore. Approaching shore we again transferred—this time to a row-boat, which in turn grounded on the shallow beach before the town; and we finally landed dry-shod on the backs of the native crew, who waded ashore.

Lindi, a town of some 4,500 native inhabitants, is about sixty miles north of the Portuguese border, and about eighty-five miles south of Kilwa (Kivenje). Lindi, before it fell into our hands, had been the southern headquarters of the Pro-

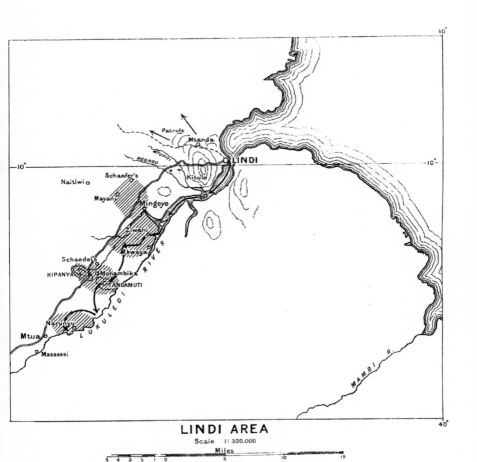

LINDI AREA

Scale 1:300,000

Miles

5 4 3 2 1 0   5   10   15

tectorate, and at the north end of the town there is a large, stone-built fort and extensive barrack buildings. Along the shore front, facing the sea, there are a number of large, colonial, commercial buildings and residences: otherwise the town, which extends inland from the sea, is comprised of palm-shaded streets of grass-roofed, mud-walled huts, with an odd whitewashed hut inset here and there—the barter-den of an Arab or Goanese trader. Lindi is low-lying and unhealthy, as is the Lukuledi Valley, south of the town, where the broad swamp estuary of the Lukuledi River flows into the bay. Moreover, the brackish-flavoured well water of the town was very bad, and added to the tremendous difficulty that was experienced in maintaining the health of white troops in this area. Behind Lindi the ground rises to a low hill-crest, the ridge of which runs north parallel to the coast line, and it was along this crest, overlooking the roads inland, that our present line terminated. In pre-war days sisal, palm oil, and rubber had been the chief products developed in this area by settlers, and large, carefully cultivated estates were plentiful in this neighbourhood.

At Lindi we were soon fully occupied preparing for active operations. The main force of the enemy—excepting the smaller force near Mahenge under Tafel, and opposed to General Northey—were now confined to a limited area in the south-east corner of the Colony, and were facing our forces at Lindi and Kilwa. This force, under General von Lettow-Vorbeck, was estimated to be 4,000 to 5,000 strong. Against these forces a new offensive began under the command of General Van Deventer, who at the end of May relieved General Hoskins; and from June onward was carried on relentlessly, while the enemy, with their backs to the wall, as it were, fought desperately.

Behind the Kitulo Hill, which rose immediately west of Lindi, lay a broad flat swamp through which crossed the Mtupiti and Ngongo Rivers on their course to the Lukuledi estuary.

Across this waste the enemy were holding a strong line, on a nine-mile front, in the rubber plantations and bush, with particularly strong fortifications at Schaafer's Farm and Mingoyo village on this line.

On 10th June it was decided to attack, and on that day columns left Lindi to flank widely those positions on their north and south extremes. The force to the north, which marched inland from Lindi, was composed mainly of a battalion of King's African Rifles and some artillery. The force operating south was comprised of another battalion of King's African Rifles, our own battalion—the 25th Royal Fusiliers—and South African Field Artillery. Under cover of darkness the latter force was to proceed some miles inland up the wide river estuary, and effect a landing, if possible, in the centre lagoon of the three at the head of the estuary, where a trolley line from Mkwaya terminated at a small timber landing-stage. General O'Grady was in command in this area, and the operations were carried out under his direction, and personal supervision in the field.

On the evening of 10th June, toward sundown, scenes that were strange, and that must have astonished the native inhabitants, were afoot on the water-front at Lindi. Out in the sultry, windless channel, with their bows up-stream, lay the active-looking warships H.M.S. *Hyacinth* and H.M.S. *Thistle,* while between them and shore fleet motor-boats plied busily on ordered errand. Inshore wide-beamed lighters with steam tugs in attendance lay off the end of the shallow-draught pier, while a number of large open boats, linked together in twos and threes by their bow ropes and towed by motor-craft, lay outside in the current—all in readiness to take aboard their human freight. And then, into the town marched soldiers in fighting kit; a battalion of British infantry appearing from the north, while black troops and some artillery came down from the hills: all to come to a halt in a long column on the dust-thick road on the shore front near to the pier. As dusk approached, embarkation commenced, under naval and military direction, and under orders of strict silence—and gradually the boats filled while the line on the road melted away until none remained on shore! . . . All were aboard! and we drew off shore and lay to in the bay waiting for darkness—an ominous force, in their silence that was nigh to sullenness, but in reality filled with suppressed excitement over the novelty and promise of adventure.

We had not long to wait for darkness. Soon it crept down rapidly, as is its habit in Africa. Under naval direction the craft then cast loose one by one, and the dark forms on the water, each in the wake of the other, followed silently on their way up-stream. In the lead were the patrol launches armed with machine-guns, and some of the intermediate motor-boats were likewise prepared for emergency.

Hour after hour we crept up the wide stream with black, threatening shores on either beam, and all remained quiet, and nothing stirred on land to break the stillness of the sultry night nor our pent-up expectancy. Our destination was eight miles up-stream. About half-way we passed through the narrow neck between Kombe and Kala islands, and a short time later our motor-boat, when hugging the east bank, had the misfortune to ground on a sand-bar and hold fast. While we lay there, phantom dark craft passed us, going up-stream and returning down. One heard a low, tense word or two spoken across the gloom, the muffled beat of the engines; and then the darkness swallowed everything. After some delay and much exertion with poles and oars, we got afloat again and proceeded, now more slowly, up-stream, keeping our course by following a tiny bright light, like a firefly, that showed now and again in the distance ahead, where the leaders were in the stream or had landed at an important bend in the channel.

About midnight, when we were still persistently working up the channel, which had narrowed. considerably, exclamations and low voices drifted to us out of the darkness ahead.

In a moment more we knew that we were at our destination, while voices directed us to the landing-place close on our right. It was very dark—so dark that one could at best see a yard or two—so, groping along the boat-bottom, you got near to where a voice said "jump," and in doing so found yourself immersed to your very knees in deep, holding mud through which, after you had got rifle and equipment clear of the mess, you waded heavily ashore; no longer dry and fairly comfortable, but wet, mud-plastered and chilled, and thoroughly uncomfortable.

On our arrival we learned that, at the landing, a German picket had been alarmed and driven in, and therefore we knew that the enemy command would soon be warned that danger threatened.

Back from the landing there was a long, narrow, level mud-flat, clear of the bush that bordered it blackly on either side, and here our forces formed up as they landed. Finally, when all were accounted for and in position, word was passed round that we were to remain here for an hour or two, and men stretched themselves on the hard tidal-damp ground and shivered; yet slept as only tired soldiers can sleep.

At 3 a.m. we were up and on the move again; slowly marching up the trolley line that led inland, in a southerly direction, toward Mkwaya. Breaking the stillness of a bush-land that apparently lay asleep and without inhabitant, I remember a solitary cock, at some near-by dwelling, crowed clear and full-voiced as we neared Mkwaya; declaring habitations, and promising the coming of dawn. Almost immediately afterwards the first faint shade of daylight was heralded by the boom of artillery from the direction of Mingoyo.

Overnight the monitors had moved into the estuary, and it was on H.M.S. *Thistle,* who had nosed her way far up-stream, that the Germans opened fire. Reply came immediately from the ships, and, as soon as it was full daylight, they were heavily shelling all enemy positions within range. During the action

153

H.M.S. *Thistle* received one disturbing direct hit, but not a vital one, and she remained seaworthy through the action. Aeroplanes were up all morning busily *spotting* for our guns, and observing enemy movements as best they could in the darkly screened bush.

Meantime, our turning-point had been reached at Mkwaya, and we now headed westerly in the direction of the Mohambika valley, behind Mingoyo, while the King's African Rifles, who were an hour or so in advance of us, were now well out on our left flank and moving parallel to us. Some two hours later we had reached the valley crest at Ziwani, and overlooked the Mohambika valley and across to the opposite crest where lay hidden, in the bush and forest, the large native village of Mrweka and Schaafer's Farm. Large numbers of the enemy were seen, about 1,500 yards distant, moving along the edge of the bush in rear of Mrweka, while smoke-puffs of gun-fire from the enemy artillery could be plainly seen farther down the valley toward Mingoyo. An advance was attempted down into the valley, and action thereafter commenced, but the valley was found to be almost impenetrable—a wide sugar-cane swamp in which the enemy were already located, and which they commanded from the opposite valley crest—and, as the left column were by this time heavily engaged and not making progress, we were ordered, meantime, to dig in on the Ziwani crest while the enemy kept up persistent long-range machine-gun fire on us. Enemy soon appeared to be everywhere on our front and left, for whenever patrols left the ridge and commenced descent into the valley they encountered enemy in force, and were driven in. Finally, the situation culminated when, about 2 p.m., the enemy launched a terrific attack on our left flank and attempted to storm our position. On the left the ground fell away, as in front, and they had crept up the valley side in the grass and bush, until no more than thirty yards from our line—when their fire burst on us like a thunder-clap. From then on one lost all reckoning of time, all reckoning of everything, except that there was something big on that kept every energy alive and working at fever speed. In the end, toward night, we had won, and won handsomely; finally routing the foe from their offensive at the point of the bayonet, and capturing two of the three machine-guns which they had in the line. To add one final trial to this grim encounter, hives of bees had been shot down from the trees during the action, and their inmates descended on us at the end of the day in infuriated swarms to drive us almost crazy with the agony of their stings. They inflicted such punishment that many men could barely see through their half-closed eyelids on the following day, while everyone suffered from cruel yellow-poisoned face scars.

The attack had been a tremendously bold venture on the part of the enemy, who were, for the present, under Von Lettow in person, apparently in large and even superior force in the neighbourhood, and it gives an idea of their strength and desperation, and the game-ness of their fighting—which one cannot help but admire. Had we been native troops, the result of such a daring blow might have been different; and even as it was, one looked back and thanked God for one thing—and that was that, even at point-blank range, the enemy's shooting had been bad, for their deadly sweep of fire was, in general, too high. Had they got the correct elevation, their machine-guns alone were sufficient to deal terrible havoc along our short, hastily and half-entrenched line.

Meantime the column in the bush—wide on our left—had met with opposition that they could not well break through; and no word had come in from the inland column that was operating in the north, which was momentarily expected to converge on to the position across the valley, and relieve the pressure on that side; and so, for the night, there was nothing for it but to hold on where we were.

One had here a striking example of the difficulties of bush operations; of the disappointments, of the almost impossible task of keeping in touch with each force, across wide areas of dense, untouched, unfamiliar bush miles ahead of the base. One never knows, at the commencement of a day, the full difficulties to overcome; one can never altogether foresee the obstacles that will be encountered to enforce delay, be it an impassable swamp, impenetrable forest, an un-bridged river, a loss of direction, or an unknown enemy force. It has been called a difficult campaign; but the difficulties have been so gigantic that the wonder one has is that the men who direct it have not grown old and grey with the weight of the anxieties imposed.

Next morning, too late, the force on the north occupied Mingoyo and Mrweka, for overnight, under cover of darkness, the enemy had evacuated their positions, and had fallen back on their second line of defence across the trolley rails at Mohambika village.

The battalion remained the day at Ziwani, and the following day, leaving other troops to hold the line, we crossed the valley and proceeded by stages, overland, back to Lindi. The enemy force, through the sudden appearance of new companies on this front, apparently now outnumbered ours, and it was, it appeared, necessary to hold on and recuperate our forces, as far as possible, which were becoming increasingly difficult to keep up to reasonable establishment owing to overwhelming sickness and lack of proportionate reinforcements. Also, our column was operating in conjunction with the Kilwa column, which had a much longer distance to advance before both would close in on Massassi, the enemy base of operations. Therefore those causes accounted for our again *holding on* for a period at Lindi.

On 15th June we were again back in Lindi. A week later the battalion was experiencing a fell wave of coast fever, which thinned our ranks at an appalling rate. On 26th June the S.M.O. inspected the men remaining on duty, to inquire into their general physique and endeavour to trace the plague to any local fault, and at that time less than half our fighting strength were on parade. Other units were suffering in similar manner, but were losing men somewhat less rapidly. Next day camp was moved to higher ground, above Lindi, but though sickness abated it still continued to find daily victims, and it was heart-breaking to be thus weakened of our fighting strength; more especially as we were not long returned from our rest at the Cape, which it had been thought would surely resuscitate our health for further campaigning. But looking back now it is apparent that the hardships of the first two years in Africa had sapped far more than the mere surface strength of the men, and the short change, though it brightened everyone outwardly, had not time to repair completely the debilities of thoroughly exhausted systems. Moreover Lindi, and the Lukuledi valley, were undoubtedly the most unhealthy country it was ever our misfortune to enter, and we had been in more than one bad area in the past.

On 1st July I received orders to take up a position on Mtanda Plateau, with fifty rifles and two machine-guns, and there to establish an outpost one and a half mile from Lindi on the Noto Road, defending the approach on Lindi from the north-west, and north, where coast tracks led away to Kilwa, on which the enemy might retire, from before the Kilwa column, and here congregate. Mtanda Plateau was a broad ridge, overlooking Lindi and the sea from its south-east bank, and, crossing to the other side, where the ground again fell away to low country, its north-west aspect overlooked great distances of hill-broken, bush-covered country. The plateau was a jungle of breast-high grass and low bush, within a forest of stately mango trees.

Routine on the outpost was to have strong, alert pickets posted near the road at night, and, through the day, to patrol the country out before us, sometimes to an outward-bound distance of ten miles. In view of the possibility of a night attack, on one or two dark nights the monitor H.M.S. *Severn* experimented with her flash-lights, turning them on to our position from where she lay in the bay, and weirdly those lights lit up the jungle.

We remained twenty-four days on this outpost, but experienced in that time no untoward incident. One or two German natives came in and gave themselves up, claiming at the same time to be porters, but sometimes such deserters had the military bearing of Askaris, and no doubt were really such, and had discarded their equipment and rifle in fear of terrible punishment for having fought against us—which was a belief taught them by their white masters.

On the morning of 25th July the detachment evacuated the outpost, and rejoined the battalion at Lindi in preparation to again resume the offensive. On the 26th the battalion trekked from 4.30 a.m. until 2 p.m. via Naitiwi, to Mayani, a planters' station, having then come thirteen miles, by track, out into the country of our June operations.

We stayed a few uneventful days at Mayani, and on the night of 1st August moved on into Mingoyo, there to join the column, on the eve of an offensive against the enemy, who were holding a front which had its centre before Mohambika village, on the trolley line, its extreme north flank on Kipanya Ridge, and its extreme south flank on Tandamuti Hill: in all a front of some four miles. The next day we were in action, which I can, perhaps, best describe in quoting the following notes:

One a.m., night of 2nd August, up and getting ready to move. Left Mingoyo at 3 a.m.—our battalion, with the main column which was to operate on the left flank, and which advanced slowly through thick bush in the direction of Tandamuti Hill. Enemy first encountered about 6 a.m. Engaged in force 9 a.m. and 3/4 King's African Rifles in attack. They were a newly recruited battalion, and this was their first time in action, and the wear of attack told heavily on them, particularly when finally opposed to the fortifications on Tandamuti Hill crest. It was then that two companies of our unit went forward to reinforce

Fortification.

TANDANUTI.

↗ Direction of British Attack.

Enemy holding ridge and fort concealed in trees on summit: mobile reserves behind ridge.

the front line. They lost no time in charging the enemy position, but found themselves, ultimately, against a dense, thorn-built *boma* fence, through which they could not break and, under telling fire, they swung off to the left flank, and withdrew. The battalion machine-guns were now established fifty yards from the *boma*, after casualties had lost me four of the most able and invaluable gunners, and thenceforward the *boma* and fort were raked with heavy machine-gun fire, and shelled by Stoke's guns; until finally, about 3.30 p.m., the enemy response was completely silenced within the fort, while German bugles rapped out their rallying calls in the valley in the rear of the hill. But orders were now received to retire, as the other two columns on the right had been held up; in fact, the central force, operating immediately south of the trolley line near to Mohambika, had even been forced to retreat, by weight of the numbers opposed to them. This was indeed a day brimful of adventure and expectancy, while everyone was aware of the great strength opposed to us, and the desperation of the fighting. But this was not the end of it. Soon after commencing the retirement heavy firing broke out in our original rear. It transpired that Kraut, in command of a company, had broken into our line of communication, and had attacked and scattered the whole of the 1st-line transport porters and their escort. The defenceless porters had flung away their loads and fled, leaving everything to the mercy of the enemy, and we encountered inconceivable disorder on the baggage-littered track when we came along. But, just before reaching this point, we, too, were pounced on by an ambush on the left, and terrific firing again ensued until the enemy were driven off. We then came to the advanced Field Hospital, where it was found the German raiders had entered, and even had had the audacity to order the native orderlies to supply the German whites with tea, while they removed all the quinine and such medicines of which they were in need. But the whites had treated the wounded with consideration, and, with revolvers drawn, had ordered their wildly excited blacks to stand clear of any possibility of interference. Finally we marched wearily into Ziwani, to camp about 11 p.m., very tired after being twenty-two hours on our feet. So ended another day of battle, one of hard fighting and heavy casualties, and one which goes to show that at periods we had not got it all our own way by force of numbers, nor by superior fighting qualities, and that the final defeat of the enemy was the result of many a hard knock, given and taken. As General Van Deventer said, later, in a dispatch dated 21st January, 1918:—"The completion of the conquest of German East Africa could only be brought about by hard hitting and plenty of it"—which has, has it not? much of the theory which General Foch had on the battle-fields of France. On 9th August preparations were again afoot to resume the offensive, and a column under Colonel Taylor—which contained, in part, the remnants of the 8th South African Infantry, lately landed in Lindi from farther up the coast—left about midday to strike east into the Lukuledi River, and, thence, southward, to be in a position to outflank widely Tandamuti on the following day.

On 10th August our force advanced up the Mohambika Valley in touch with the trolley line, which was on our right. At evening we camped west of the old Tandamuti position, having passed Mohambika village and come to our halting-place without encountering any sustained resistance. . . . On the morning of this day at 7 o'clock, and again recommencing at 1 p.m., Tandamuti Hill was heavily shelled by the long-range guns of the monitors *Severn* and *Mersey*, from where they lay up the river estuary some eight to ten miles to the north-east, and also by the howitzers of the Royal Garrison Artillery, and the field guns of the South African Artillery. And this cannonade, and the threat of impending attack of the same severe nature as in the preceding week, apparently decided the enemy's retirement, for by the evening we had advanced and were in possession of all the positions which we had fought so hard for a week before. Next day, but now leaving the trolley track and striking deeply into the bush, the advance continued, and during the forenoon we joined in with the left column, which then preceded us in a southerly direction, through tall grass and much bad bush. Light engagements occurred from time to time with the advance guard, but the column kept moving on, though progress was painfully slow, while every new aspect of the country ahead was being carefully investigated, for well was it known that any 100 yards of fresh ground might hold an ambush and a trap. At the end of a wearisome day we reached the Lukuledi River, where it flows for some miles on a course due east, and then camped about 1½ mile west of Narunyu, which was reported occupied by the enemy.

12th August—Thoughts recall the grouse moor, and this day of days at home, but again it passes with but memories. All porters have gone back to bring forward rations, while we halt here near Narunyu.

From 13th August to 18th August we remained closely in one area, where low hills and ridges encompassed us on all sides. West of us the enemy had established a line defending the approach to Narunyu, and our line dug in before them, while engagements daily occurred here and in the neighbourhood, and we were fitfully subjected to shelling by the enemy's artillery.

The weather at this time broke down, and we had five consecutive days of heavy rain, which, as we had no blankets or grass-hut shelters, made us very cold, wet, and miserable, while during the nights we slept lying in rain-soaked mud—a condition of things that brought out even more fever than usual.

18th August—Overnight, under cover of darkness, part of our forces evacuated camp and travelled northerly, and then westerly, until we drew in to the trolley line: then we lay down and waited until early morning. At 3 a.m. we were moving again, and the column had crossed the open avenue of the trolley line, and were lost again in the bush, before daybreak. All morning we moved, through truly terrible thorn-bush country, in a south-westerly direction, thereby widely circling round to attack the Narunyu position from the west, while our other forces, at the camp we had left, would hold the enemy's attention on the east. About 11 a.m., when drawing in to the hill-crest overlooking Narunyu, which is situated in a valley bottom, the first-second King's African Rifles, in the lead, encountered large forces of the enemy, and entered into action. On their establishing a firing line, the rear of the column was drawn in, and a perimeter was formed, for, in the thick bush we were then in, attack might threaten from any direction. This was a wonderfully wise and fortunate precaution, for no sooner were our lines on all sides established than the enemy opened a determined attack on our right flank; and, as the fight continued, fierce and sustained attacks developed later, even in our rear and on our left. In other words, the enemy were all around us and trying to break through our *square* in the bush. It was a day of tremendous battle. There were, within the circle, the first-second King's African Rifles, 25th Royal Fusiliers, and Stoke's Guns, and back to back they fought, without one minute's cease in the deafening fusillade, until long after dark. It was here that one saw, and realised, the full fighting courage to which well-trained native African troops can rise. The first-second King's African Rifles was one of the original pre-war regular battalions, and magnificently they fought here; and we, who were an Imperial unit, felt that we could not have wished for a stouter, nor a more faithful, regiment to fight alongside of. About 8 p.m. the firing ceased and we had at last a breathing space and could hear each other speak in normal voice. But all was not yet over. At 9.30 p.m. an enemy whistle blew sharply—and instantaneously a great burst of enemy fire swept the square from the right flank, and from closer quarters than before. An enemy force had crept in in the darkness and silence, and tried to take us by surprise.

163

But they reckoned wrongly, and in the end, after a fierce encounter, they were driven off and silenced: though movement and groans, from beyond our front, continued long into the night while the enemy collected their dead and wounded.

There was now opportunity to review the situation and its vital points: the King's African Rifles were very short of ammunition, and it was felt that the situation might become serious in the event of a sustained night attack—what ammunition could be spared was handed over to them by our battalion.

Casualties, after such extremely heavy fighting, were not excessively heavy, which was undoubtedly due to the lie of the ground, for our position was in a slight dip that could not be detected from the enemy lines. We were out of touch with G.H.Q. and the reserve column, and a patrol was sent out to try to get through to Headquarters, though we had now no fear of joining up, for we had confidence we could hold on, and had in the fighting worn down the enemy's will to strike. *Water* was our greatest need—there was none within our square.

At last our anxieties ceased. Weary, powder-blackened, mud-filthy, thirsty beyond the telling, the line slept fitfully through the remainder of the night.

Dawn found everyone standing to, and patrols investigating the bush out in front of the lines. Some patrol fighting took place close in, but the enemy trenches of yesterday were found to be evacuated, and the enemy line now some 700 yards away on our right flank and front. At 9 a.m. General O'Grady arrived in camp, and relief was felt that we were again in communication.

Heavy fighting had been experienced at all points yesterday, and casualties of comrade acquaintances, in other units, were learned of with regret.

It was decided that we were to hold on here, and arrangements were made to bring water to camp, while bully and biscuit would be our ration—no tea, no cooked food, for no fire could be allowed on account of the smoke, which would have marked our position to enemy artillery. The enemy were shelling the square and shooting dangerously close, but were unable to locate us exactly, or tell where their shells were landing, in the dense bush. Today all ranks were very exhausted after the past week of blanketless, half-sleepless nights and the extreme strain of yesterday.

For five days we lay in the confined square in our shallow trenches, drinking sparingly of foul water, and holding impatiently on, while smaller engagements went on with the enemy, who continued to invest our front closely and right flank. Our porters had a bad time here. In time cooked food was sent up for them from the rear, but on the first two days it was common to see the poor creatures hungrily munching their uncooked ration of hard rice-grains. At the end of the five days, many of them were almost unable to walk, and could not be burdened with an ammunition load.

On 22nd August our battalion received orders to withdraw under cover of night to the reserve column at the main camp back some miles on the trolley line and west of Tandamuti—a camp which was designated C.23.

The withdrawal was quietly accomplished, and at 9.30 p.m. we camped at C.23. And then we had, what in the past few days we had come to dream of—tea, tea, tea. Camp-fires were started everywhere, and we sat there and feasted our fill of tea that tasted threefold more fragrant and delicious than ever before, and on cooked food, warm and palatable, and long we sat into the hours when weary heads should have been asleep.

We remained at C.23 until 4th September, and at intervals each day were shelled by the enemy's long-range guns, at aggravating intervals.

A large camp had sprung up at C.23, and additional forces and additional stores were daily arriving. But we were in terribly unhealthy country; the air was close and oppressive, and the sun merciless; and men went about their duties with list-less bearing. The hospitals were full of sick, and troops and porters were being evacuated in hundreds every few days. The native African was suffering as much as if not more than the European. The 25th suffered no less than other units, and our forces were sadly growing smaller and smaller.

On 4th September the battalion left C.23 and advanced to the centre and left camps before Narunyu, to occupy the front line there; relieving the 8th South African Infantry, who were tottering with sickness and unfit for further service in active fields.

Here utter physical exhaustion, and fever, which had gripped me for some time, began slowly to master endurance. For a few days I struggled on, having just enough strength to "stand to" by the machine-guns in the early mornings, and afterwards to direct the day's routine. Those days were com-monplace—there was sometimes some exchange of firing at daybreak, and on some occasions the camp was shelled; while we were gratified to see considerable numbers of porter and Askari deserters come in and give themselves up.

On 5th September we had news that the Kilwa column had progressed considerably and were at Mssinoyi River on 4th September, sixty miles south-west of Kilwa, and some 110 miles off their ultimate objective—Massassi.

On 9th September I had not strength to walk, and later in the morning I was taken to hospital. I was beaten, hopelessly overcome, though no man likes to give in. General O'Grady came to see me when I lay on my stretcher at the Field Hos-pital—perhaps the bravest man I have fought under, and the kindest—and, in my weakness, when he had gone, I hid my face in the gloom of the low grass hut and broke down like a woman. I had worked under his direction many times, on reconnaissance and other special work, when he was Chief of Staff, and when he commanded a brigade, and now he was sorry I was *done*—and I, ah well! my heart was breaking because I could not stay on, as he and the last of my comrades were doing.

There remains little more to add. By stages I was transported by ambulance to Lindi, and thence by sea to Dar-es-Salaam, where at the end of September I lay for a few days dangerously ill, and was pulled through only by the tireless care of the doctor and sisters. On 2nd October I was borne aboard the *Oxfordshire* and sailed for South Africa.

My actual experience of the German East Africa campaign thus ended. The Lindi column were, at the time of my departure, reinforced by the Nigerians, and fighting of the same severe nature as I have described, against Von Lettow and his concentrated forces, continued 1½ month more in the fever-stricken Lukuledi Valley before the Kilwa and the Lindi forces effected a junction.

Not long after that was accomplished, on 25th and 26th November, Von Lettow avoided final surrender by crossing the Rovuma River south-west of Massassi, and escaped up the Luyenda River into Portuguese territory; while Tafel's force—of some 2,000 to 3,000—which, too late, tried to effect a junction with the main force, was cut off, and on 28th November surrendered unconditionally.

On our side, there is one sorrowful disaster to record which touches this narrative deeply. In the final action which my unit undertook—the only one after my departure—the remnants of the band, steel-true men who had come through everything till then, were pitted against overwhelming odds, when covering a retirement, and fought till they were cut to pieces.

It was a tragic ending.

CHAPTER 8

Nature Notes

It would be difficult to picture East Africa without her vivid abundance of nature, for it is "the creatures of the earth" that for ever astonish all who enter this country of vast wildernesses and few habitations of white men.

In this connection I will endeavour to describe some of the forms of wild life that were most closely associated with camp and trek during the campaign.

To begin with, if I may bring them into the category of wild things, there were the natives of the country—who aided us tremendously during the campaign, and without whose aid it would have been well-nigh impossible for our columns to traverse the country. Broadly speaking, we had to deal with four distinct types of native—the Swahili-speaking tribes, the Kavirondos, the Kikuyus, and the Masai. The Swahili-speaking natives, whose tribes were numerous and included such fighting peoples as the Whahamba, Diruma, and Nandi, were most generally recruited from the coast areas; they were the most intelligent and adaptable natives in our service. Many of them made splendid Askaris, while as trained porters, for machine-guns, signalling sections, and stretcher-bearers, they were extremely useful, and many thousands were utilised for such work. Those natives were extraordinarily keen on their drills—in which they were daily instructed, whenever opportunity arose, to ensure combined movement without confusion, and quick obedience to orders—and it was a common thing to see them, after a parade had been dismissed, continue their drill within their own lines, under the direction of one of their enthusiastic headmen. They were simple, good-natured people, those blacks, and very easy to deal with if one took the trouble to understand them and their language, and ruled with a strong yet considerate hand. But they were unfortunate, and at a loss, when they came under the charge of strangers who had not had opportunity to understand them or their language—which often occurred, owing to loss of experienced men through sickness or casualties, and their replacement by men freshly arrived in the country.

When we entered German territory many Swahili natives, of the inhabited districts we passed through, were hired by all ranks as personal servants, and thenceforth became followers of the column. Those were usually boys of from fifteen years to twenty-five years. They subsisted on any kind of diet, and often foraged for scraps in camp and for fruits in the bush, with much of the instinct of animals.

Those who were ignorant were taught to cook, and to do the many little duties of body-servant; and were a great boon to trek-tired men when camp was reached and they were available to cut grass for the bed on the ground, fetch water, kindle camp fires, and help in the cooking of food.

The Kavirondos from the Lake District, and the Kikuyus from the Nairobi area, were used almost exclusively for carriers and camp cleaners, and were perhaps less intelligent than the average Swahili native, and of lower type. Nevertheless, some of them were very useful, and I have used picked men from both tribes as higher-grade machine-gun porters, and found them come very close to the standard of the good Swahili.

The warlike nomad Masai roamed the upland grass-lands of their great reserves and held aloof from warfare. Only as guides in the early days on the frontier were they of usefulness to our forces, and at that time they were often seen about our camps. They were remarkable for their knowledge of direction in a country of few apparent landmarks, and for the speed at which they could cover long distances, with their ungainly shuffling run.

I turn now to the big game of the country.

I know no more interesting and wonderful sight than that we often witnessed, and that may be today witnessed, on the Kajiado Plains, and in the neighbourhood of the Guaso Nyero valley. Not even the wonderful migration of the vast bands of caribou in the far Canadian North can surpass the sight of game one will see here in a day. In a single day's march herd after herd of game may be passed feeding plainly in view in the open grass veldt—herds of wildebeest, hartebeest, zebra, and Grant's gazelle, are the most plentiful; and small groups of Thomson's gazelle, oryx antelope, giraffe, and ostrich. While in the Guaso Nyero valley it may be your good fortune to sight a large herd of buffalo.

Eland antelope I only remember seeing in two localities— at Maktau on the frontier, and in the Rufiji valley.

Within German territory no such vast numbers of game were encountered: but that may have been because we did not again travel through open veldt of the same nature as contained the herds on the frontier. Most game, in German territory, were seen in the low-lying Mgeta and Rufiji valleys. At Tulo and Kissaki, some species of game were plentiful. At Tulo, reed-buck, water-buck, impala, and wart-hog were numerous, while a number of hippopotamus haunted the sluggish Mwuha River. At Kissaki, bush-buck, Harvey's duiker, and wart-hog were the principal small game, while here, and out to the great Ruaha and Rufiji Rivers, the territory was renowned for elephant.

Elephant tracks, old and new, were everywhere in the neighbourhood of Kissaki, but animals were seldom seen, since they were very wary, and extraordinarily quick in scenting danger. If they detect human scent—which they will pick up a mile

OSTRICHES.

or more down-wind—they are at once alarmed and fast travel away from the danger, very often covering great distances before reassured that they have reached a zone of safety.

At the Rufiji River a remarkable number of hippopotamus were seen. North of Kibambawe village there is a chain of lakes no great distance apart, and I have passed one of those lakes, Lake Tágalala, when there have been scores of hippo, visible in the water. I should think the marsh-banked Rufiji River throughout its course teems with those strange, cumbersome, uncomely animals.

Rhinoceros were perhaps most plentiful on the frontier, and were often encountered when patrolling the thick bush, or bush-covered hill-country. During the many times I have met those animals at close quarters—and I have stumbled across as many as four separate animals in a single night when on particular reconnaissance—I have never known them to charge seriously when not wounded. I have experienced them rush straight on to the sound of a stick crackling underfoot, but, when they drew close and got my wind, they veered off instantly to one side, and escaped in the bush rapidly and fearfully. I remarked my experiences to Selous, for they were not what I had been led to expect, and he corroborated them by saying that he also had never seen one charge a man when unmolested.

Selous, too, in discussing lions, in his quiet, practical way, laid very little stress on the dangers of hunting those animals. He said there was little danger of their ever venturing to attack unless wounded, and then the greatest danger was in going into long grass to search for an animal that in all probability would be lying there concealed, and at bay, and ready to spring on an over-hasty pursuer. Selous's advice was that, "in hunting lions you should try to get a clean clear shot at your quarry, at fairly close quarters, and to shoot to kill with your first shot." "Don't attempt snapshots and wild shooting, which only lead to a bad hit, and a dangerous lion at bay to be dealt with."

The eerie roar of lions was often heard at night outside our camps, or near to the bivouac of a lonely outpost, and sometimes, through the day, they were seen by our outlying pickets; but I only know of three being shot by members of our battalion during our service in East Africa.

I turn now to the bird life of the country. In the bush, in the neighbourhood of water, birds, of various kinds, were often plentiful, and were remarkable, as a rule, for their brilliant plumage. But they were seldom conspicuous in numbers in the open, for, as a rule, they kept closely within the cover of the bush and jungle grass; and on this account I have often heard unobservant men remark on how little bird life they saw during the campaign in East Africa. Their unobtrusiveness, too, was added to by the fact that very few African birds are songsters.

I think the bird most commonly seen throughout the campaign was the red-eyed turtle dove *(streptopelia semitorquata),* and their soft cooing in the quiet evenings was certainly the outstanding note of bird life in the country. It is a truly African sound—a sound which one who has heard it will always associate with African fantasy—and which sometimes strikes the ear as most pleasant and soothing, and, at other times, haunts you with its persistent hint of native sadness.

A more remarkable call, but only heard in certain localities, was the strange bottle-bubbling echoing call of the lark-heeled cuckoo—a largish partridge-barred brown bird with a long tail—which was usually uttered at dark, or through the night, by a lone bird perched somewhere on the topmost twig of an outstanding bush or tree, sending his soft note-clear call out over the ocean of misty leaf-tops ; where it would be picked up and responded to by another like sentinel at some other distant signal-post.

The most common bird to enter our encampments was the white-necked raven, a bird similar in habit and colour to the British rook, but with a large white mark on the nape of the neck. He was   the chief scavenger of our camps, though, sometimes, he was ably aided by the Egyptian kite, one, or a pair, of which species was commonly with us.

Common varieties of the neat little mouse-like wax-bills were, on occasions when we were near to permanent habitations, the only *sparrows* to visit camp.

In odd hours, when the chance occurred, I, and one or two others who became interested, collected some specimens of bird life, chiefly with catapult and trap, in the absence of better weapons, and, notwithstanding the difficulties of storage and transport of the skins, at the end of the campaign had secured the specimens below recorded; which, along with a collection of butterflies, eventually, by purchase, passed into the magnificent collection in Lord Rothschild's museum at Tring, where such splendid scientific research in world-wide zoology is being extensively and actively prosecuted.

The correct nomenclature of all species has been very kindly formulated by Dr. E. J. O. Hartert, Director of the Tring Museum.

This was, under the circumstance of soldier life, but a small collection, but it is interesting to note that they proved useful and of interest. Dr. Hartert wrote concerning them:

Nos. 1 and 26. It is surprising that a new species should still be found in British East Africa. It seems, however, probable that the specimens mentioned by Reichenow from Ugogo as probably—judging by the somewhat poor description and figure in the Proceedings of the Zoological Society—being *serinus donaldsoni,* are not the latter, but this new species, which I have described as *serinus buchanani* at the January meeting of the British Ornithological Club, 1919. I have compared the specimens with the types and other examples of *s. donaldsoni* in the British Museum, from Somaliland, and it is evident that *s. buchanani* differs by its larger and less curved bill, longer wing, and more yellowish colour, especially the sides being yellow with faint stripes, not green with black streaks.

LIST OF SPECIES COLLECTED

Name of Species.	Sex.	Where Secured.	Date.	Reference No.
WADERS				
Plover, Ringed (*Charadrius hiaticula hiaticula*) . . .	♂	Maktau, B.E.A.	25.10.15	30
Stilt (*Himantopus himantopus himantopus*) .	♂♀	Bura, B.E.A.	29.12.15	81
Sandpiper, Common (*Tringa hypoleuca*) .	♀	Maktau, B.E.A.	27.9.15	12
HERONS, STORKS, ETC.				
Hammerhead (*Scopus umbretta bannermani*) .	♂	Bura, B.E.A.	29.12.15	82
Heron, Buff-backed (*Bubulcus ibis ibis*) .	♂	Moschi, G.E.A.	9.4.16	110
PIGEONS				
Pigeon, Hartert's Green (*Treron calva brevicera*) .	♀♂	Moschi, G.E.A.	12.4.16	115, 116
Pigeon, Rameron (*Columba arquatrix arquatrix*) .	♂♀	Kibosho, G.E.A.	1.5.16—5.5.16	147, 150, 154, 155
Pigeon, Crimson-winged (*Turturoena delegorguei harterti*) .	{juv.}♀♂	Kibosho, G.E.A.	7.5.16	160
Dove, Tamburine (*Tympanistria tympanistria fraseri*) .	♂♂	Moschi, G.E.A.	16.4.16	128
„ Red-eyed Turtle (*Streptopelia semitorquata semitorquata*)	♀	Lindi, G.E.A.	6.7.17	218
GAME BIRDS				
Guinea-fowl, Crested (*Guttera pucherani*) .	♂	Kirengwe, G.E.A.	2.12.16	210

BIRDS OF PREY

Hawk, Lesser Barred (*Kaupifalco monogrammicus meridionalis*)	♀	Lindi, G.E.A.	25.6.17	216
Eagle, African Crested (*Lophoaetus occipitalis*)	♂	Bura, B.E.A.	23.12.15	78
„ Steppe (*Aquila nipalensis orientalis*)	♂	Kissaki, G.E.A.	30.11.16	209
Buzzard, Steppe [*Buteo buteo rufiventris* Jerd. [= *anceps*, Brehm]	♂♀	„ „	30.10.16	183
Falcon, African Lanner (*Falco biarmicus biarmicus*)	♀	„ „	14.11.16	196
Falcon, Pigmy (*Poliohierax semitorquatus*)	♂	Maktau, B.E.A.	7.11.15	45

OWLS

Owl, Great Eagle (*Bubo lacteus lacteus*)	♀	Tulo, G.E.A.	26.9.16	171
„ Spotted Eagle (*Bubo africanus africanus*)	♂	Lindi, G.E.A.	7.7.17	219

PARROTS

Parrott, Meyer's (*Poicephalus meyeri* Matschiei) (Remarkable yellow variety)	♀	Namanga, G.E.A.	2.3.16	85
„ Brown-headed (*Poicephalus fuscicapillus*)	♀	Lindi, G.E.A.	9.7.17	221

PLANTAIN EATERS

Plantain Eater, White-bellied, Grey (*Schizaerhis leucogastra*)	♂	Bura, B.E.A.	22.12.15	77
„ Hartlaub's (*Turacus hartlaubi*)	♂	Moschi, G.E.A.	22.4.16	138

CUCKOOS

Cuckoo, Lark-heeled (*Centropus superciliosus superciliosus*)	♀♂	Bura, B.E.A.	16.11.15	49
„ „ „	♂		14.12.15	69
Coucal, Southern Green (*Centhmochares aereus australis*)	♂♂	Kirengwe, G.E.A.	20.11.16	202
Cuckoo, Golden (*Chrysococcyx cuprius* [= *cupreus* auct.]		Bura, B.E.A.	18.11.15	50
			14.12.15	
„ Klass's Golden (*Chrysococcyx klaasi*)	♂	Lindi, G.E.A.	11.7.17	222

Name of Species.	Sex.	Where Secured.	Date.	Reference No.
BARBETS				
Barbet, Black-winged (*Lybius melanopterus melanopterus*)	♂	Moschi, G.E.A.	16.4.16	125–130
,, Yellow-vented (*Lybius torquatus irroratus*)	♀	Kissaki, G.E.A.	15.11.16	197, 198
,, Spotted-breasted (*Tricholaema stigmatothorax*)	♂	Maktau, B.E.A.	19.9.15	3
,, Pied (*Tricholaema lacrymosum*) ,,	♂♀	Moschi, G.E.A.	27.9.15	10–11
Tinker, Small (*Barbatula pusilla affinis*)	♂	,,	3.1.16	95
Barbet, Böhm's (*Trachyphonus darnaudi böhmi*)	♀	Bura, B.E.A.	3.1.16	84
,, White-cheeked (*Smilorhis leucotis kilimensis*)	♂	,,	11.12.15	57, 58
	♀	Moschi, G.E.A.	27.4.15	142
WOODPECKERS				
Woodpecker, Bearded (*Mesopicos namaquus*)	♀	Kirengwe, G.E.A.	20.11.16	203
,, Masai Cardinal (*Dendropicos guineensis massaicus*)	♀	Moschi, G.E.A.	8.4.16	106
,, Hartlaub's Cardinal (*Dendropicos guineensis hartlaubi*)	♀?	Kissaki, G.E.A.	9.11.16	192
COLIES				
Coly, White-headed (*Colius leucocephalus*)	♂	Maktau, B.E.A.	1.11.15	36
,, White-cheeked (*Colius striatus affinis*)	♂	Bura, B.E.A.	12.12.15	62
,, ,,	♀	Moschi, G.E.A.	5.4.16	101, 108
	♂		8.4.16	
ROLLERS				
Roller, Lilac-breasted (*Coracias caudatus caudatus*)	♂	Moschi, G.E.A.	9.4.16	112
,, Cinnamon African (*Eurystomus afer suahelicus*)	♂♀	Maktau, B.E.A.	6.12.16	40
,, ,,	♂	Kissaki, G.E.A.	7.12.16	212

HORNBILLS

Species	Sex	Locality	Date	No.
Hornbill, Crested (*Bycanistes cristatus*)	♀+♀+♀	Moschi, G.E.A.	30.4.16	145
,, von der Decken's (*Lophoceros deckeni*)		Maktau, B.E.A.	31.10.15	32
,, Crowned (*Lophoceros melanoleucus suahelicus*)	♀	Moschi, G.E.A.	1.5.16	149

KINGFISHERS

Species	Sex	Locality	Date	No.
Kingfisher, Hooded (*Halcyon leucocephala leucocephala*)	♂+♂+♀	Bura, B.E.A.	14.12.15	68
,, Lesser Brown Hooded (*Halcyon albiventris orientalis*)		Moschi, G.E.A.	28.4.16	143
,, Striped (*Halcyon chelicuti*)	♂+♂+♀	Makindu, G.E.A.	29.7.16	167
,, Painted (*Ispidina picta picta*)		Moschi, G.E.A.	14.5.16	163
,, Crested (*Corythornis cristata*)	♂ ?	Bura, B.E.A.	19.12.15	74

BEE-EATERS

Species	Sex	Locality	Date	No.
Bee-eater, Little Yellow-throated (*Melittophagus pusillus cyanostictus*)	♂	Maktau, B.E.A.	2.11.15	39
,, Southern Little Yellow-throated (*Melittophagus pusillus meridionalis*)	?	Bura, B.E.A.	4.1.16	85
Bee-eater, Southern Little Yellow-throated (*Melittophagus pusillus meridionalis*)	♂	Kissaki, G.E.A.	21.10.16	178
Bee-eater, Cinnamon (*Melittophagus oreobates*)	♂+♀	Moschi, G.E.A.	28.4.16	144
,, Olive-Green (*Merops superciliosus*)		Lindi, G.E.A.	8.7.17	220

HOOPOES

Species	Sex	Locality	Date	No.
Hoopoe, Wood (*Irrisor erythrorhynchus marwitzi*)	♂	Lindi, G.E.A.	6.7.17	217

NIGHTJARS

Species	Sex	Locality	Date	No.
Nightjar, Inornated (*Caprimulgus inornatus*)	♀+♀	Makindu, G.E.A.	5.12.15	55
,, Fosse's (*Caprimulgus fossii fossii*)		Lindi, G.E.A.	12.7.17	223

Name of Species.	Sex.	Where Secured.	Date.	Reference No.
SWIFTS				
Swift, Palm (*Tachornis parvus myochrous*)	♂ young	Kissaki, G.E.A.	18.10.16	176
SWALLOWS				
Swallow, Common European (*Hirundo rustica rustica*)	♂	Maktau, B.E.A.	31.10.16	31
" Lesser Stripe-Breasted (*Hirundo puella*)	♂♀	Moschi, G.E.A.	1.4.16	88
" Ermin's Red-breasted (*Hirundo emini*)	♂	" "	7.5.16	157
" Wire-tailed (*Hirundo smithi smithi*)	♂♀	Kibosho, G.E.A.	2.4.16	90
" " "	♂	" "	21.4.16	137
" " "	♀	" "	1.5.16	148
FLYCATCHERS				
Flycatcher, Neumann's Scrub (*Bradornis neumanni*)	♂	Maktau, B.E.A.	7.11.15	46
" Mouse-coloured Scrub (*Bradornis pallidus murinus*)	♂♀	Makindu, G.E.A.	28.7.16	166
" Littoral Puff-backed (*Batis molitor littoralis*)	♂♀?	Maktau, B.E.A.	7.11.15	47
" Puff-backed (*Batis molitor puella*)	♀♂	Bura, B.E.A.	12.12.15	64
" " "	♀	Moschi, G.E.A.	15.4.16	121, 122
" Wattle-eyed (*Platysteira peltata peltata*)	♂♀	Kirengwe, G.E.A.	21.11.16	207
" Suaheli Paradise (*Tchitrea perspicillata suahelica*)	♂	Moschi, G.E.A.	16.4.16	126
SHRIKES				
Shrike, White-headed Crow (*Eurocephalus rüppelli deckeni*)	♀ juv.	Bura, B.E.A.	18.12.15	72
" Helmeted (*Sigmodus retzii*)	♂	Narunyu, G.E.A.	2.9.17	226
" Yellow-spotted Bush (*Nicator gularis*)	♂	Kirengwe, G.E.A.	19.11.16	119
" Black-fronted Bush (*Chlorophoneus nigrifrons*)	♂♀	Moschi, G.E.A.	19.4.16	141

SHRIKES (Continued)

	♂ ♀			44-48
Shrike, Red-breasted (*Rhodophoneus cruentus cathemagmenus*) .		Makindu, G.E.A.	7.11.15—18.11.15	
,, Sombre (*Laniarius funebris funebris*) . .	♂♂	Maktau, B.E.A.	18.9.15	2
,, Lesser Sombre (*Laniarius funebris degener*) .	♂♂	Moschi, G.E.A.	7.4.15	105
,, Black-and-White Bush (*Laniarius aethiopicus aethiopicus*) .	♂♂	,, ,,	13.4.16	119
,, Grey-headed Green (*Malaconotus poliocephalus approximans*)	♂♀	Lindi, G.E.A.	16.7.17	224
,, Lesser Puff-backed (*Dryoscopus cubla suahelicus*) .	♀♂	Moschi, G.E.A.	9.4.16	111
,, ,, ,, ,,	♀♂	Makindu, G.E.A.	30.7.16	169
,, Great African (*Lanius cabanisi*) . .	♂♀	Maktau, B.E.A.	24.10.15	29
,, Fiscal (*Lanius collaris humeralis*) .	♀♀	Moschi, G.E.A.	8.4.16	107
,, Black-crowned Bush (*Harpolestes senegalus orientalis*) .	♂♂	Bura, B.E.A.	18.11.15	52
,, Lesser Three-streaked Bush (*Harpolestes australis*) .	♂♂	Kissaki, G.E.A.	6.11.16	185

DRONGOS

	♀			165
Drongo (*Dicrurus ater lugubris*) . . .	♀	Makindu, G.E.A.	28.7.16	165

ORIOLES

	♂			151
Oriole, Lesser Black-headed (*Oriolus larvatus rolleti*) .	♂	Moschi, G.E.A.	3.5.16	151

STARLINGS

				158,159
Starlings, White-bellied, Glossy (*Cinnyricinctus leucogaster verreauxi*)	♂♀	Moschi, G.E.A.	7.5.16	158,159
,, Stuhlman's Lesser Red-winged (*Stilbopsar stuhlmanni*) .	♂♀?	,, ,,	7.5.16	156

WEAVERS, WAXBILLS, WHYDAHS, ETC.

				51
Weaver, Black-headed (*Ploceus nigriceps*) . .	♂♀	Bura, B.E.A.	18.11.15	51
,, Cabanis' Yellow-Black (*Ploceus melanoxanthus*) .	♂♂	Maktau, B.E.A.	7.11.15	43
,, Golden (*Ploceus aureoflavus aureoflavus*) .	♂♂	Kissaki, G.E.A.	8.11.16	189
,, Uniform Gros-beak (*Amblyospiza unicolor*) .	♀	Kirengwe, G.E.A.	21.11.16	205

Name of Species.	Sex.	Where Secured.	Date.	Reference No.
WEAVERS, WAXBILLS, WHYDAHS, ETC. (*Continued*)				
Bishop, Red-crowned (*Pyromelana flammiceps*)	♂	Kissaki, G.E.A.	15.10.16	172
Finch, Hooded Weaver (*Spermestes scutata*)	♂	Moschi, G.E.A.	18.4.16	133
Waxbill, White-spotted (*Hypargos niveoguttatus*)	♀	Kirengwe, G.E.A.	19.11.16	200
Finch, Melba (*Pytelia melba*)	♂ juv.	Makindu, G.E.A.	30.7.16	168
(or Kirk's?) (*Pytelia melba belli* [or *kirki*])	♀	Kirengwe, G.E.A.	21.11.16	204
Waxbill, Mozambique (*Estrilda astrilda cavendishi*)	♀	Kissaki, G.E.A.	22.10.16	181
,, Little Ruddy (*Lagonosticta senegala ruberrima*)	♂	Moschi, G.E.A.	18.4.16	136
,, Violet-bellied (*Uraeginthus ianthinogaster hawkeri*)	♂	Maktau, B.E.A.	6.10.15	17
,, Bengali (*Uraeginthus bengalus niassensis*)	♂	,,	1.11.15	35
,, Northern Bengali (*Uraeginthus bengalus schoanus*)	♂	Kissaki, G.E.A.	18.10.16	177
Whydah, Pied Pintail (*Vidua serena*)	♀	Moschi, G.E.A.	26.4.16	140
	♂	,,	16.4.16	129
FINCHES				
Sparrow, Suaheli, Grey-headed (*Passer griseus suahelicus*)	♂	Moschi, G.E.A.	4.4.16	97
	♀	,,	17.4.16	131
Finch, Hartert's Serin (*Serinus maculicollis harterti*)	♂	Maktau, B.E.A.	25.9.15	6
,, Buchanan's Serin (*Serinus buchanani*)	♀	,,	18.9.15	1
	♂	,,	9.10.15	26
Siskin, Spotted African (*Spinus hypostictus*)	♀	Moschi, G.E.A.	15.4.16	123
,, ,, ,,	♂	,,	18.4.16	132
WAGTAILS AND PIPITS				
Wagtail, African Pied (*Motacilla vidua*)	♀	Moschi, G.E.A.	3.4.16	92
,, Long-tailed Pied (*Motacilla clara*)	♂	,,	3.5.16	152
Pipit, Golden (*Tmetothylacus tenellus*)	♂	Maktau, B.E.A.	1.11.15	38

LARKS

Lark, Masai Sabota (*Mirafra poecilosterna*)	♂♀♀	Matau, B.E.A.	15.10.15	24
,, Foxy (*Mirafra alopex*)	♂♀	,, ,,	19.10.15	25
,, ,,		,, ,,	31.10.15	33

BULBULS

Bulbul, Greater Green Forest (*Andropadus insularis insularis*)	♀♂♀	Kirengwe, G.E.A.	21.11.16	206
,, Yellow-vented (*Pycnonotus barbatus micrus*)	♂♀	Moschi, G.E.A.	3.4.16	96
,, ,,		,, ,,	12.4.16	113

SUNBIRDS

Sunbird, Little Collared (*Anthreptes collaris elachior*)	♂♀♀♂♀♂	Kissaki, G.E.A.	21.10.16	179
,, Lampert's Senegal (*Cinnyris senegalensis lamperti*)		Moschi, G.E.A.	31.3.16	86
,, Yellow-bellied (*Cinnyris venusta falkensteini*)		,, ,,	4.4.16	93
,, Bifasciated (*Cinnyris bifasciata microrhyncha*)		Kissaki, G.E.A.	1.4.16	87
,, Kilimanjaro Long-tailed (*Nectarinia kilimensis kilimensis*)		,, ,,	18.10.16	173
		Moschi, G.E.A.	13.4.16	117

WARBLERS

Warbler, Red-headed Grass (*Cisticola ruficeps scotoptera*)	♂♂♀	Maktau, B.E.A.	29.9.15	14
,, Dwarf Grass (*Cisticola nana*)		,, ,,	8.10.15	18
,, Common Grass (*Cisticola lateralis*)	♀♂♀	Moschi, G.E.A.	6.4.16	102
,, Uniform Wren (*Calamonastes simplex simplex*)		Maktau, B.E.A.	10.10.15	20
,, Long-tailed Scrub (*Prinia mistacea tenella*)	♂♀	Kissaki, G.E.A.	9.11.16	194
Crombec, Jackson's (*Sylvietta*) [probably *jacksoni*] ♀ juv.	♀	Moschi, G.E.A.	7.4.16	103
Warbler, Yellow-bellied Bush (*Eremomela flaviventris abdominalis*)	♀♂♀	Maktau, B.E.A.	10.10.15	21
,, Golz's Long-tailed Forest (*Euprinodes flavidus golzi*)	♂♀♂♀	,, ,,	8.10.15	19
		Kissaki, G.E.A.	9.11.16	191
Babbler, Aylmer's (*Argya aylmeri mentalis*)	,, ,,	Maktau, B.E.A.	26.9.15	8
,, Kirk's (*Crateropus kirki*)		Moschi, G.E.A.	14.4.16	120
Whinchat, African (*Saxicola torquata axillaris*)		Kibosho, B.E.A.	8.5.16	161
Wheatear, European (*Oenanthe oenanthe*)	♂♀♂♀	Maktau, B.E.A.	28.9.15	13
,, Pileated (*Oenanthe pileata*)		Moschi, G.E.A.	4.4.16	98

The nest of *s. buchanani* was found at Maktau in the fork of a thorn tree about eight feet above the ground, on 26th September, 1915. It is a somewhat flat structure of fibres and rootlets, interwoven with cobwebs and wool. The three eggs are pale blue with purplish black dots and short lines around the wide pole. They measure 20 by 14·8 and 19·3 by 14·7 mm. They closely resemble the eggs of the trumpeter bullfinch.

(init.) E. H.

No. 13, *Oenanthe oenanthe* (European wheat-ear) collected at Maktau, B.E.A., on 28th September, 1915. This appears to be an early date for the occurrence of the European wheat-ear so far south.

(init.) E. H.

No. 36. *Colius leucocephalus* (white-headed coly). This species is still very rare in collections. It is at once distinguished from all other colies by its well-marked white head.

The first example was obtained by Fisher at Wapokomo, B.E.A., in 1878, and long remained a unicum. The trader Abdu Jindi sold a skin from Bardera to the Paris Museum. The British Museum possesses specimens obtained on the Guaso Nyero, B.E.A., by Lord Delamere, and by Atkinson at Logh, Somaliland. The late Baron Erlanger collected five specimens in Southern Somaliland. The bird is figured in *Coliidae,* Genera Avium 6, 1906. Quite recently Zedlitz received three males and one female from Afgoi, South Somaliland.

(init.) E. H.

No. 105. *Laniarius funebris degener* (lesser sombre shrike), collected at Moschi, Kilimanjaro Area, is from a locality that is remarkable. Hitherto only known from South Somaliland, but agrees perfectly with *degener,* being smaller than *atrocaeruleus,* and much less deep black than *l. funebris funebris.*

(init.) E. H.

Nos. 115, 116. *Treron calva brevicera* (Hartert's green pigeon). In *Novitates Zoologicae,* 25. 1918, I have, with the help of

Arthur Goodson, reviewed the African green pigeons of the *calva* group. We were able to distinguish not less than nine subspecies, and there seem to be one or two other, still doubtful ones, in N. E. Africa. In the *Catalogue of Birds* in the British Museum all these nine forms were united, while Reichenow separated two, and recently four different ones. The specimens from East Africa have given us the greatest trouble. It is evident that a distinct form with a very short naked *cere* or basal portion of the beak, and with a sharply defined lavender-grey nuchal collar, is found in East Africa around Kilimanjaro and thence to the Athi River, Machakos, Matabato Hills, and to the Kikuyu Mountains and Escarpment. This form we called *treron calva brevicera.*

(init.) E. H.

No. 152. *Motacilla clara* (long-tailed pied wagtail). This is the bird which used to be called for many years *motacilla longicauda,* but as this name had been preoccupied, Sharpe named it *motacilla clara* in the fifth volume of the *Band-list of Birds.*

(init.) E. H.

I collected also during our travels some specimens of plants for Dr. A. B. Rendle of the British Museum, and was fortunate to secure some interesting species, four of which were new, and not formerly recorded, and have been described in the *Journal of Botany* (October, 1916), while others, unfortunately, were too fragmentary to determine, or to give more than a genus name, though nine of them are possibly new species.

The East African plants obtained were:

CAPPARIDEAE
  Cleome hirta Oliv.

PORTULACACEAE
  Talinum cuneifolium Willd.

TILIACEAE
  Grewia canescens A. Rich.

GERANIACEAE
  Pelargonium sp.

LEGUMINOSAE
  Vigna fragrans Bak. fil.
  Rhynchosia sp.

RUBIACEAE

Pentas carnea Benth. (forma)
Oldenlandia Bojeri Hiern

COMPOSITAE

Erlangea Buchananii S. Moore
(sp. nov.)
Vernonia Hoffmanniana S.
Moore
Vernonia lasiopus O. Hoffm.
Ageratum conyzoides L.
Notonia abyssinica A. Rich.
Wedelia abyssinica Vatke
Melanthera Brownei Sch. Bip.
Senecio disciflorus Oliv.
Berkheyopsis diffusa O. Hoffm.
Aspilia, sp.
Achyrocline luzuloides Vatke
Zinnia multiflora L. (New
World plant ; an escape
from gardens.)
Erythrocephalum longifolium
Benth.
Triplocephalum Holstii O.
Hoffm.
Mikania scandens Willd.
Pluchea dioscoridis DC.
Polycline (sp. nov. ?)

OLEACEAE

Jasminum Buchananii S.
Moore (sp. nov.)

APOCYNACEAE

Adenium coetaneum Stapf

ASCLEPIADACEAE

Daemia extensa R. Br.
Sarcostemma viminalis R. Br.

BORAGINACEAE

Cynoglossum lanceolatum
Forsk.

CONVOLVULACEAE

Ipomaea Wightii Choisy
Hewittia bicolor Wight

SOLANACEAE

Solanum panduraeforme E.
Mey.

SCROPHULARIACEAE

Rhamphicarpa Heuglinii
Hochst.
Rhamphicarpa serrata
Klotzsch. var. *longipedi-
cellata* Engl.
Striga elegans Thunb.

GESNERIACEAE

Streptocarpus caulescens Vatke
(Ulugúru Mts.)
Streptocarpus sp. (Ruwu
River)

PEDALINEAE

Sesamum (sp. nov. ?)

ACANTHACEAE

Thunbergia affinis var. *pul-
vinata* S. Moore
Thunbergia alata Bojer
Barleria maculata S. Moore
(sp. nov.)
Ruellia, sp.
Eranthemum Hildebrandtii
C. B. Clarke
Ecbolium namatum C. B.
Clarke
Barleria, spp.
Barleria ramulosa C. B. Clarke
Somalia (sp. nov.).
Blepharis linariaefolia Pers.
Justicia Fischeri Lindau

VERBENACEAE

Priva leptostachya Thunb.

LABIATAE

Leucas, sp.
Erythrochlamys spectabilis
Gürke
Coleus decumbens Gürke
Plectranthus burúensis S.
Moore (sp. nov.)
Leucas leucotricha Baker

NYCTAGINEAE
  Boerhaavia plumbaginea Cav.
  Boerhaavia pentandra Burch.

AMARANTACEAE
  Aerua lanata Juss.
  Aerua brachiata Mart.
  Digera arvensis Forsk.
  Centema rubra Lopr.

CHENOPODIACEAE
  Chenopodium album L.

EUPHORBIACEAE
  Phyllanthus amarus Schum. &
  Thonn.

(Species possibly new when genus only is given.)

BRITISH MUSEUM (NAT. HIST.)
30th *May*, 1916.

A. B. RENDLE.

In collecting in this way, in odd hours, one was constantly moving about, and to that, strange as it may seem, I ascribe my good fortune in keeping fit and free of sickness during the first two years of service in the tropics. I feel sure, even if one feels listless and exhausted, that it is a mistake to lie about camp in the oppressive heat when off duty, pestered by flies and camp dust, and brooding over your discomforts. Some of the men of the battalion became interested in this searching for curious things, and, after a time, it was noticeable that they were the ones most contented with the hardships they endured, and among the fittest on trek. Africa had undoubtedly the power to depress men's spirits in no light manner, and thus, to find something to do and think about, in any interval of idleness, was a good thing.

Lastly, I will refer to the pests of camp-life and trek.

The common house-fly was a terrible pest at all times. They swarmed over everything, and were a particular source of annoyance when food was being prepared, or being eaten. It was impossible to take steps to reduce their number in the limitless areas through which we were constantly passing, and there was nothing for it but to endure the plague, while, whenever camp was established for a few days, all rubbish was scrupulously burned or buried so that they would have as little to attract them to our neighbourhood as possible.

A large glossy *blue-bottle*—following the ghastly trail of dying transport animals, was also a common and disease-carrying pest. When the elephants—mentioned previously—were shot in the Ulugúru Mountains, they were miles from any habitation, and in vague bush country, which one would judge was no habitat of *blue-bottles*, yet in an hour they were in millions on the dead carcases—so many that the standing grass was weighed down with the blackness of flies settled on each stem. The sense that brought such swarms to one small centre in so short a time is beyond understanding. Should a horse die on the roadside, but a day will elapse before it becomes a seething mass of *blue-bottle* larva and terrible to look upon.

Mosquitoes, in regard to their irritating bite and their nocturnal activities, were, on the whole, not very troublesome, and in no instance have I a record of their being particularly bad, but they carry the malaria germ, and, in that they did so, they were our most deadly enemy. As protection against them everyone was supposed, by S.M.O. order, to sleep beneath mosquito net, but that was often quite impossible when trekking, and our kit miles in rear.

In some parts we passed through, especially if riding, the tsetse fly was a terrible pest, for they bite hard and deep, and follow you persistently on your way for many miles. It is that fly which is credited with carrying the germ of that dread disease sleeping sickness—while, as is well known, its bite is particularly fatal to imported horses and mules, and, in lesser degree, to cattle.

Ants, too, were among our enemies. And once you have been amongst red fighting ants in long marsh grass you are never likely to forget them. Sometimes, too, those species trek during the night, and I have seen a sleeping camp turned out in the middle of the night by those insects swarming over everyone and biting furiously. And, after a day of hard trekking, this kind of disturbance is very far from pleasant, as may be judged by the vicious exclamations of abuse that arise out of the darkness. These red ants were the worst of their tribe, and many an uncomfortable experience we had with them. Again, there was a tiny species of ant that was always with us. It infested every article of our belongings, and particularly anything edible, and on that score was a great nuisance, though quite harmless otherwise. As if there was not enough to plague the life of man, spiders, tarantulas, and scorpions on occasions found their way into your blanket, and they were insects that were dreaded, for their stings were very painful and poisonous and inflamed and irritated the part afflicted for days.

There are a great many bees in East Africa, and the natives place hives for them in the trees and collect the wild honey from time to time. These bees, if annoyed, are the most dreadful insect in Africa. On two occasions hives were disturbed by our battalion, and swarms of the annoyed inmates descended to inflict terrible punishment on all those in the neighbourhood. On the first occasion their attack was more than human flesh could endure, and an entire company was routed in disorder from the neighbourhood. I have never before seen bees attack with such ferocity nor sting so poisonously. On the first occasion of attack one unfortunate man was completely overcome, and lay on the ground groaning and screaming, while bees were apparently biting him to death. From this he was rescued, but not before he was mentally unbalanced, and had to be removed to hospital. On the second occasion of attack another individual suffered almost equally severely.

Many snakes were killed about camp, but no one of our battalion, so far as I know, was ever seriously bitten by one. One python was killed and a number of puff-adders, and a great many of the smaller grass snakes. I have seen men, when sleeping in the open, awake at daylight to find a snake, 4 to 6 feet long, curled against their body for warmth, but, on being disturbed, they slid off quietly into the grass, and were gone without attempting to be antagonistic.

At Kissaki camp we experienced a bad plague of mice. At the time we were there, the entire neighbourhood had been burnt out by the natives in clearing their cultivated ground of undergrowth, and this had driven the mice into camp. There were thousands of them—they lived in your grass roof by the score, they scuttled about the floor of your hut o' nights, and while you slept they played "hide and seek" over your blankets. It was a common thing for half a dozen biscuit-tin traps—makeshift traps made by ingenious Tommies—to catch a hundred mice in a night.

Those are but brief references to the forms of nature that were closely associated with the campaign; some giving us pleasure, some adding to our trials and discomforts—but all memorable to those who have bivouacked and trekked under the tropic sun.

CHAPTER 9

Here and Hereafter

WAR

War is as a storm of the clouds—a human storm. Dark frowning clouds, commotion and strife, and outbursts of thunder—and before the threatening disaster we tremble, and hope and fear.

It is the changing of the Universe, this mighty upheaval within nations, and there is the impulse of destiny in it. As a storm will clear the atmosphere, afterwards there will be sunshine and better things. Not for today, and the present, is this warring of nations, but for the future, and the wisdom of those who in generations will follow us.

Was not the world growing fast into a plaything? Something in the form of a pleasure-giving empty bubble, growing larger, floating uncertainly, the surface substance—that which is visible to the eyes and mind—transparent, and weak, and unworthy of the clear and vigorous world from which it had risen, brightly coloured, and to which it was fast descending, colourless and vague. As a bubble will burst, so was a climax imminent.

Does not war, this drastic liberation of opposite forces, hold for us a lesson? Are we not passing through the throes of upheaval to change the mind of our race from vanity to wisdom? The world today is steeped in blood and sorrow; and all the suffering would be in vain, were there not hope that the world will arise in the end sobered, and humbled, and eager to live anew.

WAR MATERIAL

Is not to enter war to enter an arena of great possibilities, wherein a great game may be played, or a bad game? But, in any case, it is so closely and seriously fraught with terrible issues that it bares the character of men to the very bone. And there are many characters—not one character, but a thousand characters; some great, some small, some active, some dormant, but out of all such elements it is a wise man's wish to weld a universal organisation of strength; and an ignorant man's folly to look at no other ambition but his own.

And therein lie the factors of all troubles of organisation, and the tremendous internal difficulties of army or national construction. One man—or body of men—may plan to build well, but can only succeed if the material is good: if the material is bad, there results failure, with credit neither to the builder nor the material. And human character is material— the most delicate material great builders may know and direct, in war, or commerce—just so many human beings prone to be directed so far, and for the rest to rise or fall, in the world's estimate, as our characters decide. But out of this mass of human character, out of these manifold qualities of a multitude, is formed the final whole which goes to mark the characteristics of an era of history, and a national greatness or littleness.

Like unto axe-men felling trees in a forest is the destructive hand of warfare. The land is depopulated of its finest timber, and that which will take a lifetime to replace. Wholesale destruction reaches far beyond the actual crime of killing. It breaks the evolution of growth, retards or destroys the life-history of a species, and leaves, through the age it occurs in, an irreplaceable blank in the population and wealth of a country.

This is not the first war, nor has anyone in the present authority to state that it is the last. If war and the felling of our forests must be, it is well to cling stoutly to the old features of the race and cultivate, in place of the fallen giants, clean-limbed sturdy saplings of full-worthy quality to serve the generations of the future.

It will concern us greatly in the future to cultivate a race strong enough to endure the buffeting of great elements, and true and straight as the best of the race of the past. For the country will want a race that is fine-grained and sure-rooted, and fit to stand up against the stress of the many storms of a restless world's brewing.

How little we are, we pawns of a universe: how far-reaching is war in the destruction of our plans! At the beginning of life it has picked us up in its whirlwind, from every stage of life, and left our poor ambitious castles in the air, tiny long-forgotten dust-heaps on the plain.

And yet we laugh and hide our sorrow, and go on, on our new-found task, our future now no farther ahead than we can see, and trusting in God that all will come right in the end.

We learn at the front and at home that nothing else matters, that nothing really counts in the greatness of a nation but clean, unshaken, sacrificing purpose, and ceaseless industry: worthless are all our little deceits and vanities, and greed of personal gain.

That nation will find religion and prosperity which holds on to the deeper lessons of war, long after war is over. To forget those lessons will be to sin against God and conscience, and the great silent grave-yard of our dead, who died that their nation might live.

Industry will greatly concern us after the war. On that will our nation depend for its solid existence hereafter, as it does today, on the activities of our war-worn, long-enduring men-at-arms. We should be glad that there will be much to do, for work is a fine thing. It is sincere in its object—it accomplishes, and it satisfies the strongest trait in our character: that wish of all men to establish a stable place of existence where they can support an acknowledged standing of manhood.

Had we not to provide for ourselves, the chief care of our lives would be taken away from us. In idleness we would become brainless and degenerate. Nature has decreed her purposeful laws of all existence. Everything that lives must industriously seek to find its means of livelihood, and its means of defence against its enemies. For instance, in wild nature, do not birds and animals without cease spend all their lives providing themselves with food, and defending themselves against storms and their enemies? In similar manner so must we; so must all things.

THERE ARE CENTURIES OF TIME

The world is very, very old, and a mighty universe in which a man is but an infinitesimal activity of creation. After all, in spite of the breathless, concentrated ambitions of a lifetime, we are a little people and we only live on earth for a very little while. Let us then, above all, make our fireside, and that of our neighbours, as pleasant as we can. For love and beauty have a powerful influence to promote the better religion, the stronger manhood of our race, and it is those intimate characteristics, wisely planted, that may take root and grow, and be everlasting long after we have travelled over the line and are gone.

It is sometimes our misfortune to misunderstand the scene or the life around us. Forgetting our humility, it is often our temperament to find fault, rather than reason, with the picture we view; and fault-finding causes uneasiness, pain, and strife.

Perhaps our first care should be to perfect ourselves, and, next, to harmonise with the endeavours of our neighbours. It would be well to go pleasantly forward to find the best that is in anything—to look for the little gleams of beauty which throw light across most pictures, no matter how dark the background.

Some men, like a giant moth in its full beauty of life when it breaks from its chrysalis cell, fail to accomplish anything before they are lured to the bright lights of the lamps of civilisation. Like an unfortunate moth to a lamp, it is their fate to be inevitably drawn towards the attraction, to seek an elusive something, and a possible happiness. Persistently they damage their manhood and their strength in trying to reach a luminous star within the radiant unattainable circle. Again and again they return to flutter madly to their doom; and have no wish to stay away. Until, at last—unless the will and mind overmaster the weakness, and they go soberly away—the body drops to the darkness, wasted and broken, and lies seriously damaged or dead. Ah, the pity of it!—the sadness! There lies a creature of unknown possibilities come to untimely grief.

Some men have no luck. Why are the strong impulses of a character born in a creature without the one great saving grace of control? It is the mystery of life, and it is impossible to criticise justly the man or the ultimate end. It would be wise and kind to be very generous to all acts and to all characters, since it is, above all else, "Destiny that shapes our ends." The moth could not damage its wings if the lamps were not there, and alight, and yet for generations they have hung in their places by the custom of our race, if not by the will of our God.

Judge no man hastily or harshly. Know a man long enough and, in most cases, you will know him, in some phase of life, do an act of nobleness.

Environment has a great and often a deciding influence on man's behaviour; and sometimes it is a man's misfortune never to have had a chance.

Justice is not so straightforward as it seems. To bring blame home to the true offender, or the true origin of offence, is often a task beyond human breadth of mind and human skill. We attempt, as best we can, what is God's work—He who sees and knows all things.

It is not always what appears on the surface that really

counts; it is when the storms of battle are at their bitterest that the true materials are found out, and the pure metal most praised.

How thoroughly in us is instilled the knowledge of right and wrong! How clearly we know our wickedness when we err! That alone should be sufficient to prove that there is a God and a sound foundation to religion.

Sleepless night—the bare hard ground an awkward resting-place, and our look-out on the outer edges of outer civilisation. Over on the left of camp a tireless, cheerful youngster, with spirit undaunted, is holding the long, dreary watches through the night. Once he was a dandy-dressed youth of a great city. He has come through a lot since then, he has learned his lesson and his position in a grim world of naked realities. He has risen from nothing to become a man—stripped of the fine clothes of his drifting butterfly days, and aware now of how little they were. For him the war has held more than loyalty to his country, for it held for him, in its own time, and in its own way, the finding of himself.

A boy changed to a man, and the man seeing a world that is not as he built it. He has sighed and fretted for lost dreams, but he knows the battle-ground of Life's conflict must be in the arena before him, and, headstrong and vigorous, he accepts the challenge against strange weapons and foes, and is of the stun-to prove that he has grown to be a worthy defender of his race.

ROUTINE

At your post there are some days when mists are in your eyes, and you cannot clearly see; there are days when mountains must be climbed with aching limbs and burdened back; and there are days when you are humbled in wretchedness, and glad of the kindliness of natives. Those days we all experience, but, thank God, there are days when the sky is blue and sunshine is in everything, and it is good to be alive.

Eighty per cent, of the rank and file are good fellows, glad to do their best if treated with consideration; humanity, and a little love. They are all very human, and you cannot prevent them from thinking in a human way. What they expect and desire is a strong command that lays down a just and reasonable order of things, and carries them through without confusion and change. To supply such command is often difficult—for, again, it is human nature that has to be dealt with.

Perhaps thirty per cent, of young officers are in part ignorant or forgetful of their trust and its bearing on good or bad organisation. They are sometimes inclined to imagine themselves set on a pedestal above the rank and file, spending more thought than should be on rivalling one another for rank, and stylishness, and a well-catered mess, while their men go forgotten, and left to look after themselves.

One may truly say that one does not always find strong men in large majorities down the list of young officers of a battalion—men who have a prolonged determination and ambition to endure the hard fight for a complete, wholesome, and wholly dangerous and united force. Here and there one may pick out the strong men, who never lose their military interest and who will brave anything, and then look at the remaining line which clearly shows, in the chain which is to bind the whole of a battalion, some weakness of strength, and the full extent of our failing.

It is a chain of some usefulness, thank God, but not capable, with its weaknesses, of everlasting service, nor as strong as it might be if time and material had allowed of a faultless welding.

By nature it is impossible to find all men of equal resolution, but at the same time we of some means and education are often a thoughtless people inclined to travel the line of least resistance in a difficult, self-seeking world. And that is where, in part, the fault springs from—the country from which we draw our stock has falteringly halted or fallen back in producing men of refinement and chivalry, and has encouraged in its stead a temperament of peculiar self-set vanity.

In a strong commander, a man who is loved by his men, you will always find there is refinement and generosity and bravery, and little selfish vanity—whether he be gentle-born or not. And look on the men who play the clean, straight game in any field of life, and one cannot fail to see that they are loved of all true-minded humanity. It is, they know, the only game to play, the only game that wins a mighty battle.

LEADERSHIP

The control of an ordered parade is a simple thing, and for the drill sergeant. But do not let us confuse the drill and discipline of the barrack square, which is something of an ornament and impressive, with the state of mind and aspect of a vital battle.

Gifted leadership is that which takes hold of and controls disorder—not order. No matter what we have read and have preached about discipline, the eternal fact which human nature will put before you on the awesome field is, that we are of many tempers, that all has not been calculated or understood, and that fate or circumstance has, in part, destroyed the plan so carefully arranged before setting out.

Out of such a situation nothing can lift the force, that is confronted with difficulties, but; quick thought, speedy action, and sure command. And that is the leadership so hard to obtain.

Men essentially want strength in their leaders. They will go through fire and brimstone for a good leader, and never be at a loss. Is it not a mistake to rely too much on discipline as a factor of strength? May it not be misleading to judgement of fighting strength? Drill and discipline are somewhat automatic and ornamental, and it is just that surface which is rudely swept aside in the first shock of battle.

Drill and discipline, in moderation, are good, but one should not overdo it or overvalue it. Husband the high spirit of youth as long as one can—it is the spirit that fights a winning battle.

Above all it should be remembered that soldiers are not schoolboys, or mere tools, but men, often with high-strung feelings, who have put their lives at the disposal of their country. The British soldier is essentially a practical man; he has, in peace time, been an engineer, a boiler-maker, an electrician, a mason, a farmer, or in a score of other trades, and he does not easily lose the character of his long training; nor should we expect it. He wants to be considered seriously, and as a man. He wants to do his best, within reason, and, given a fair chance, he never fails you. And, finally, he considers he has the right, at all times, to be the keeper of his own soul.

Leadership imposes a wide knowledge of human nature, and a wide responsibility; but tact, great patience, and a durable enthusiasm will carry one far on an undertaking that is full of difficulties.

CRITICISM

A soldier said to me the other day:"I have been fifteen months out here—I may be fifteen more—I may be shot tomorrow."

To him it was a commonplace remark without a note of complaint. He merely wished to show he had had time to think of the subject he was discussing from a serious point of view.

And he had been discussing the folly, the uselessness, the narrowness, the meanness of some of the newspaper and political criticisms so rife in his home papers—the home that now he passionately hoped would emerge from bloody battle-fields purified, serious, content, and aged to a greater wisdom.

He thought some journalism at home and, incidentally,

politics had been, since the date of war, very disappointing. War had brought the golden opportunity, while the State was in trouble and distress, to raise the standard of thought to high idealism. Yet had it carried on, on the whole, as before, the chief forte criticism; sometimes uttered in weak alarm or blundering foreboding—always in attack or defence of a narrow circumstance.

And, having warmed to his subject, the soldier went on to condemn criticism—and his arguments were these:

There is far too much freedom of field given to fractious, unfounded criticism. Criticism is nearly always, in some aspect, unjust; certainly it is always unkind. For it aims at striking a down-felling blow while it hits but one surface of the many-sided views of complex humanity. The surface that is struck at may be bruised or even destroyed, if the blow be straight, but there are others of the many surfaces which will merely recoil and revolt, with cause, against the blow. And there are times when the blow misses the mark altogether, and revolt is complete from all sides.

Criticism can only be justified in two forms: when it condemns a great wrong or a grave deceit—and then we should see to it that it is our law, not criticism, that deals out judgement with certain understanding; and, in the other case, when it is uttered in good spirit with helpful purpose—and then it were more rightly called advice. Surely it is wrong entirely to condemn, in bitter and unsubstantiated speech, the thoughts and purpose of another body which dares to see a phase of life, or government, in other light, and with another brain. Were it not far better to prove by deed, by clear-sighted example—not merely by words —the value of thought? And, if the opponent be a man, he will come to thank you, and both views, in the process of discussion, will become enlightened and instructive.

If he is not 'a man' his scheme of things opposed to yours should crumble away if our laws are right, and concur with the common law of decay which decrees that ill-fed roots cannot live and flourish. Does any man do right to sit on a stool at home looking for trouble in the machinery of the nation, when millions toil in endless endeavour, his object to descry weakness or fault, or to direct to his temple of ideas, while he raises no active hand to prove his knowledge or his understanding? Is he certain of his usefulness? Does his position as a man of letters entitle him, by self-appointment, to be king of people? Is there not a more noble, if harder, method of reasoning a cause to greatness? If we are to be truly great we must see the main views together, listening to all from every human standpoint— and framing the final law with certain wisdom —for the greatness of nations must spring from absolute unity of purpose, and with an honesty near to the goodness of God. And is it not by example, by action, and thereafter with broader vision, by help and advice, that mankind should build together their fortresses of strength against the battles of today and of the future? Have you seen a grim figure, grimly occupied during an action, defending his yard of trench—which is to him his Britain's all—and dealing death with certain purpose and unshakable resolution? He has nothing to say—only by deed can he hope to hold this little yard for Britain's honour.

He has no need for criticism. He has risen beyond any fault-finding or narrowness.

He may live but today, but he lives those hours for the good and the greatness of his motherland.

Should he criticise, if he comes through, methinks his words will be measured with a new seriousness, and with warmth of comradeship more than with enmity and bitterness.

And does not that common picture show the nobleness of *action,* and its accomplishment—while criticism, ignorant and powerless, is blown back into the four winds ashamed of its fragility?

I have been a lone sentry many nights now in this distant outpost, and, like a single plover seeking out the flock, I could utter his weird, wild cry of loneliness. Love is surely the strongest motive in our lives, and ah! it is cruel, and cold, and barren without any of it. . . . Yet I carry on, though sometimes losing control of wariness and pitching among the far-off fields of dream-land in search of the old home . . . then back to this lone, wild beat as before.

Is it an untamed spirit beating its life out because it has not the saving faculty of control? Or is it lost for a time on unbeaten tracks, out of the course that it was intended to keep?

The virtue of life is not in learning to get what you want, but in learning to do without what you want; and a soldier may have to do without everything.

A motto is no good if it is only an ornament on the wall. If we live up to it, then only does it become worth while.

There is one thing greater than strength that will carry one far, and that is endurance.

It is the fate of youth, in simple trustfulness, to venture forth on the broad highway of life a dreaming idealist; and to return, if the wars, go against him, with deep-cut scars and bowed head. He knows that there are plans made otherwise than his, and that they will remain unalterable, while he must break his spirit to change, and self-denial, and humbleness.

There is something of bitterness in the struggle, but it is that bitterness which makes for deeper experience and ultimate strength, though underlain with haunting sadness.

LEONAUR

ALSO FROM LEONAUR

AVAILABLE IN SOFTCOVER OR HARDCOVER WITH DUST JACKET

DOING OUR 'BIT' *by Ian Hay*—Two Classic Accounts of the Men of Kitchener's 'New Army' During the Great War including *The First 100,000 & All In It.*

AN EYE IN THE STORM by *Arthur Ruhl*—An American War Correspondent's Experiences of the First World War from the Western Front to Gallipoli and Beyond.

STAND & FALL by *Joe Cassells*—A Soldier's Recollections of the 'Contemptible Little Army' and the Retreat from Mons to the Marne, 1914.

RIFLEMAN MACGILL'S WAR by *Patrick MacGill*—A Soldier of the London Irish During the Great War in Europe including *The Amateur Army, The Red Horizon & The Great Push.*

WITH THE GUNS by *C. A. Rose & Hugh Dalton*—Two First Hand Accounts of British Gunners at War in Europe During World War 1- Three Years in France with the Guns and With the British Guns in Italy.

EAGLES OVER THE TRENCHES by *James R. McConnell & William B. Perry*—Two First Hand Accounts of the American Escadrille at War in the Air During World War 1-Flying For France: With the American Escadrille at Verdun and Our Pilots in the Air.

THE BUSH WAR DOCTOR by *Robert V. Dolbey*—The Experiences of a British Army Doctor During the East African Campaign of the First World War.

THE 9TH—THE KING'S (LIVERPOOL REGIMENT) IN THE GREAT WAR 1914 - 1918 by *Enos H. G. Roberts*—Like many large cities, Liverpool raised a number of battalions in the Great War. Notable among them were the Pals, the Liverpool Irish and Scottish, but this book concerns the wartime history of the 9th Battalion – The Kings.

THE GAMBARDIER by *Mark Severn*—The experiences of a battery of Heavy artillery on the Western Front during the First World War.

FROM MESSINES TO THIRD YPRES by *Thomas Floyd*—A personal account of the First World War on the Western front by a 2/5th Lancashire Fusilier.

THE IRISH GUARDS IN THE GREAT WAR - VOLUME 1 by *Rudyard Kipling*—Edited and Compiled from Their Diaries and Papers Volume 1 The First Battalion.

THE IRISH GUARDS IN THE GREAT WAR - VOLUME 2 by *Rudyard Kipling*—Edited and Compiled from Their Diaries and Papers Volume 2 The Second Battalion.